Questions and Answers

MATHEMATICS
KEY STAGE 4
to A*

Mark Patmore Principal Examiner
Brian Seager Chief Examiner

SERIES EDITOR: BOB McDUELL

Contents

HOW TO USE THIS BOOK	1
THE IMPORTANCE OF USING QUESTIONS FOR REVISION	1
MAXIMISING YOUR MARKS IN MATHEMATICS	2
DIFFERENT TYPES OF EXAM QUESTION	2

QUESTIONS AND REVISION SUMMARIES

1	Number	4
2	Algebra	9
3	Shape and space	22
4	Handling data	34

ANSWERS	47

Introduction

HOW TO USE THIS BOOK

The purpose of the *Questions and Answers* series is to help you achieve the grades you want in your GCSEs. This book is designed to help all students aiming for an A or A* grade and also provides a good basis for revision for the Standard Grade of the Scottish Certificate of Education, Credit Level. The companion title to this book, *GCSE Questions and Answers Mathematics*, also contains questions which are focused on the Higher tier (A*–C) papers, and will therefore provide invaluable general practice for all students aiming for A and A*.

This book is based on the idea that an experienced Examiner can give, through exam questions, sample answers and advice, the help you need to secure success. Many revision aids concentrate on providing the facts which might have to be remembered in an exam. This book focuses on giving you invaluable practice at doing exam questions, so that you can learn to improve your exam technique.

The *Questions and Answers* series is designed to provide:

- Easy to use **Revision Summaries** which identify the important facts. These are to remind you, in summary form, of the topics you will need to have revised in order to answer exam questions. (Answers to the illustrative examples are also provided.)
- Advice on the different types of question in each subject and how to answer them well to obtain the highest marks.
- Many examples of **exam questions**, with spaces for you to fill in your answers, just as in an exam. It is best if you try the questions first before going to the answers and the advice which accompanies them. The questions are either official Exam Board questions or have been specially written by experienced Examiners who write questions for the Exam Boards.
- **Sample answers** to all of the questions.
- **Examiner's tips.** By using the experience of Examiners we are able to give advice on how your answers can be improved, and how common mistakes can be avoided.

THE IMPORTANCE OF USING QUESTIONS FOR REVISION

Past exam questions play an important part in revising for examinations. However, it is important not to start practising questions too early. Nothing can be more disheartening than trying to do a question that you do not understand because you have not mastered the concepts. Therefore it is important to have studied a topic thoroughly before attempting questions on it.

It is unlikely that any question you try will appear in exactly the same form on the papers you are going to take. However the number of totally original questions that can be set on any part of the syllabus is limited and so similar ideas occur over and over again. It certainly will help you if the question you are trying to answer in an exam is familiar and you are used to the type of language used. Your confidence will be boosted, and confidence is important for exam success.

Practising exam questions will also highlight gaps in your knowledge and understanding that you can go back and revise more thoroughly.

Finally, having access to answers, as you do in this book, will enable you to see clearly what is required by the examiner, how best to answer each question and the amount of detail required.

Introduction

MAXIMISING YOUR MARKS IN MATHEMATICS

One of the keys to exam success is to know how marks are gained or lost and the examiner's tips given with the solutions in this book give hints on how you can maximise your marks on particular questions. However you should also take careful note of these general points:

- Check the requirements of your exam board and follow the instructions (or 'rubric') carefully. Many Mathematics papers start with short, straightforward questions. You should work through them in order so that you build up your confidence. Do not overlook any parts of a question – double-check that you have seen everything, including any questions on the back page! Take time to read through all the questions carefully, and then start with the question you think you can do best.

- Get into the habit of setting out your work neatly and logically. If you are untidy and disorganised you could penalise yourself by misreading your own figures or lose marks because your method is not obvious. Always show all necessary working so that you can obtain marks for a correct method even if your final answer is wrong. Remember that a good clear sketch can help you to see important details.

- When the question asks for a particular result to be established, remember that to obtain the method marks you must show sufficient working to convince the examiner that your argument is valid.

- Do not be sloppy with algebraic notation or manipulation, especially involving brackets and negatives. Do rough estimates of calculations to make sure that they are reasonable, state units if applicable and give answers to the required degree of accuracy; do not approximate too early in your working.

- Make sure that you are familiar with the formulas at the front of the exam paper and learn any useful formulas that are not included.

- When about 15 minutes remain, check whether you are running short of time. If so, try to score as many marks as possible in the short time that remains, concentrating on the easier parts of any questions not yet tackled.

- The following glossary may help you in answering questions:
  Write down, state – no explanation needed for an answer.
  Calculate, find, show, solve – include enough working to make your method clear.
  Deduce, hence – make use of the given statement to establish the required result.
  Sketch – show the general shape of a graph, its relationship with the axes and points of special significance.
  Draw – plot accurately, using graph paper and selecting a suitable scale; this is usually preparation for reading information from the graph.
  Find the exact value – leave in fractions, roots or π and note that using a calculator is likely to introduce decimal approximations, resulting in loss of marks.

DIFFERENT TYPES OF EXAM QUESTION

There are different types of question which appear on exam papers. Questions on Mathematics papers are of two types:

'Pure' Mathematics Questions

These are usually short and are focused on one particular skill or part of the syllabus.

Example 1: Solve the equation $x^2 - 3x - 40 = 0$.

Answer _____(2)

Introduction

Structured Questions

These are the most common type of question in GCSE Mathematics papers and thus most of the questions in this book are structured questions. These questions usually have a context – that is they are about the application of mathematics to a real (or nearly real!) situation.

A structure is built into the question and, hence, into your answer. Frequently, answers from one part of a question are used in subsequent parts, but an error in, say, part (a), which may result in few, or even no, marks being obtained for that part should not result in no marks being obtained in subsequent parts, provided the incorrect answer is used 'correctly'. There are numbers in brackets, e.g. (3), to show how many marks are allocated to the various parts of a question.

Example 2: (a) Astronomers estimate that there are about one thousand million galaxies in the universe. Write this figure in standard form.

Answer _____ (1)

(b) Each galaxy contains about one hundred thousand million stars. Estimate the number of stars in the universe. Write your answer in standard form.

Answer _____ (2)

Sometimes the structure is not provided by the question and you must decide how to tackle the problem.

Example 3: The diagram shows the design for a company's logo which is to be painted on the side of a building.

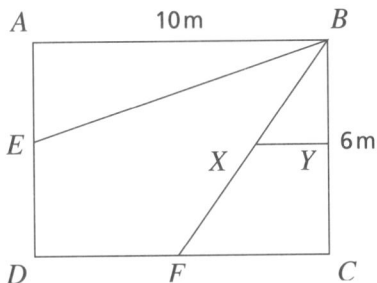

The design is a rectangle, $ABCD$, 10 m long and 6 m wide. E, the midpoint of AD, and F, the midpoint of DC, are joined to B. XY is the line joining the midpoints of BF and BC.

Calculate the area of trapezium $XYCF$.

Answer _____ m² (4)

Answers to examples:

1: $x = 8$ or $x = -5$
2: (a) 1×10^9 or 10^9 (b) 1×10^{20} or 10^{20}
3: Trapezium $XYCF$ 11.25 m²

1 Number

REVISION SUMMARY

There are two main categories in Number at this level. The first, while still involving some complicated calculation, is about the effects of **errors** in measurement upon calculated results. Care is needed when computing an error to select the appropriate upper or lower bound for each variable to maximize the error.

Example 1: The value of f is found from the formula $f = \dfrac{p}{q+r}$

The measurements are $p = 7.35$, $q = 15.2$, $r = 31.7$ correct to three significant figures.

(a) State the upper and lower bounds of p, q and r.
(b) Find the maximum error in f.

Questions asked about the other category concern **rational and irrational numbers**. It is important to be clear about the definitions. Rational numbers can be written in the form of a fraction, with whole numbers in the numerator and denominator. They therefore include numbers which are terminating decimals and recurring decimals. Other numbers which cannot be written in this way, whose decimals do not terminate or recur, are irrational. Examples of these are $\sqrt{3}$ and π.

To show that a number is rational you must show that it can be written as a fraction, for example, $0.54 = \dfrac{54}{100} = \dfrac{27}{50}$

$0.\dot{5}\dot{4}$ can be shown to be a fraction by multiplying it by 100 and then subtracting. The result is $\dfrac{54}{99} = \dfrac{6}{11}$.

Example 2: Are these numbers rational or irrational? Explain your answers.

(a) $0.\dot{2}$
(b) $0.\dot{1}\dot{2}$, that is, 0.121 212...
(c) 0.121 121 112 111 12...

Example 3: $a = 1 + \sqrt{2}$, $b = 1 - \sqrt{2}$

Are the following rational or irrational?
$a + b$, $a - b$, ab, $a \div b$.
Give your reasons.

If you need to revise this subject more thoroughly, see the relevant topics in the *Letts* GCSE Mathematics Study Guide or CD-ROM.

Answers to examples:

1: (a) 7.355, 7.345; 15.25, 15.15; 31.75, 31.65
   (b) 0.000 44 (i.e. 0.157 158... − 0.156 716... or 0.156 716... − 0.156 276...)

2: (a) rational: $\dfrac{1}{5}$ (b) rational: $\dfrac{12}{99} = \dfrac{4}{33}$ (c) irrational: does not recur

3: $a + b = 2$, rational;
   $a - b = 2\sqrt{2}$, irrational;
   $ab = -1$, rational;
   $a \div b = -3 - 2\sqrt{2}$, irrational (found by multiplying top and bottom of the fraction by $(1 + \sqrt{2})$)

Number 1

QUESTIONS

1 Angela is going to sow grass seed on a small field. She has estimated the lengths of the sides (in metres) and the angles shown in the diagram:

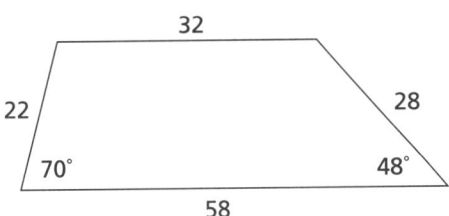

(a) Show that the field is approximately a trapezium.

   ....

   .... (5)

(b) All the measurements are correct to the nearest whole number. Angela has seed for 1000 m². Can she be sure that this is enough? Show your calculation.

   ....

   .... (4)

2 The formula $S = \dfrac{F}{A}$ is used in engineering.

   $F = 810$, correct to 2 significant figures.
   $A = 2.93$, correct to 3 significant figures.

   (a) For the value of F, write down

      (i) the upper bound, _____

      (ii) the lower bound. _____ (2)

   (b) For the value of A, write down

      (i) the upper bound, _____

      (ii) the lower bound. _____ (2)

   (c) Calculate (i) the upper bound and (ii) the lower bound for the value of S for these values of F and A. Write down all the figures on your calculator display.

   ....

   ....

                                  (i) upper bound = _____

                                  (ii)lower bound = _____ (4)

1 Number

QUESTIONS

(d) Write down this value of S correct to an appropriate number of significant figures.

_____ (1)

ULEAC 1995

3 (a) Write down an irrational number which lies between 4 and 5.

.... (1)

(b) N is a rational number which is not equal to zero.
Show clearly why $\frac{1}{N}$ must also be rational.

....

.... (2)

NEAB 1995

4 Kris ran a 400 m race in 49.4 seconds. If the time was measured to the nearest 0.1 seconds and the distance is measured to the nearest metre, what is the maximum value of his average speed, in metres per second?

....

....

Answer _____ m/s (3)

5 Write down a value of x for which $x^{\frac{1}{3}}$ is

(a) rational,

.... (1)

(b) irrational.

.... (1)

WJEC 1995

6 (a) Write down a rational number between 1.2 and 1.25.

_____ (1)

(b) Write down an irrational number between 1.2 and 1.25

_____ (1)

ULEAC 1995

Number

QUESTIONS

7. **Do not use a calculator when answering this question.**
   All working must be shown.

   (a) Write down an irrational number between 6 and 8.

   .... (1)

   (b) Show clearly why $3.8\dot{4}$ is a rational number.

   ....

   .... (3)

   (c) Given that $a = \sqrt{2}$, $b = 2\sqrt{3}$ and $c = \sqrt{6}$, determine whether each of the following expressions are rational or irrational.

   (i) $ab + c$

   .... (2)

   (ii) $(ab + c)^2$

   ....

   .... (2)

   (iii) $\dfrac{bc}{a}$

   ....

   .... (2)

   WJEC 1995

8. (a) The length of a rectangle is measured and is found to be 8 cm with a maximum possible error of 0.1 cm. Its length is written as 8 ± 0.1 centimetres. The width of the rectangle is 6 ± 0.1 centimetres. If the perimeter of the rectangle is given as 28 cm, calculate the maximum possible error in this value.

   ....

   .... (2)

   (b) A rectangle measures $l \pm a$ centimetres in length and $w \pm b$ centimetres in width. The formula $P = 2(l + w)$ is used to calculate the perimeter, P, of the rectangle. Find an expression for the maximum possible error in P.

   ....

   .... (2)

   WJEC 1995

1 Number

QUESTIONS

9 Some of these numbers are irrational. In each case, show how you decided whether it was rational or irrational.

(a) 3.142

.... (1)

(b) $1.\dot{6}$

.... (1)

(c) $\left(\sqrt{3}\right)^3$

.... (2)

(d) $\left(1+\sqrt{3}\right)\left(1-\sqrt{3}\right)$

.... (2)

(e) $\dfrac{1+\sqrt{3}}{1-\sqrt{3}}$

.... (3)

10 David travels from Manchester to London in $3\tfrac{1}{2}$ hours, measured to the nearest half hour. The distance from Manchester to London is 200 miles, measured to the nearest 10 miles.

(a) Complete these two inequalities:

3.25 hours < David's time < _____

_____ < Distance from Manchester to London < _____ (3)

(b) Calculate upper and lower bounds for the average speed for David's journey. Give these bounds correct to 3 significant figures where appropriate.

....

....

Answer Upper bound _____ mph

Lower bound _____ mph (4)

MEG 1995

Algebra 2

REVISION SUMMARY

There will be questions in this section on the manipulation of algebraic expressions and the solution of equations.

Example 1: Simplify $\dfrac{1}{x-2} + \dfrac{1}{2x+3}$

Example 2: Solve the equation $3x^2 - 2x - 7 = 0$.
Give the solutions correct to 4 significant figures.

The last part of this section is concerned with graphs. You may be asked
- to solve equations by graphical means;
- find the gradients of curves by drawing tangents;
- find the area under a curve and explain its significance;
- sketch graphs of functions.

Example 3: This is the graph of $y = f(x)$.

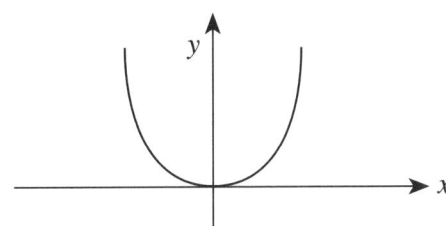

Sketch the graphs of $y = f(x + 1)$, $y = f(x) + 1$.

Answers to examples:

1: $\dfrac{3x+1}{(x-2)(2x+3)}$

2: $x = 1.897$ or -1.230

3:

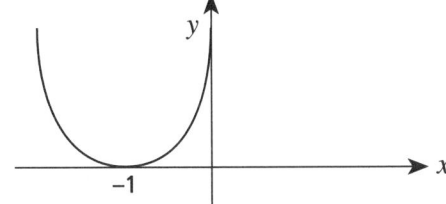
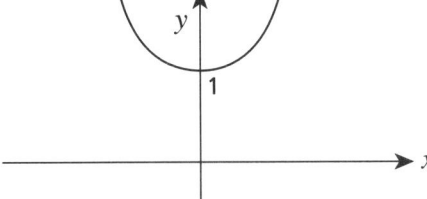

If you need to revise this subject more thoroughly, see the relevant topics in the *Letts* GCSE *Mathematics Study Guide* or CD-ROM.

2 Algebra

QUESTIONS

1 1, 2, $1\frac{1}{2}$, $1\frac{3}{4}$, $1\frac{5}{8}$, ...

(a) Explain how to get the next term.

.... (1)

(b) Investigate whether or not this sequence converges and, if it does, find the limit.

....

....

....

Answer _____ (4)

2 Pipes with equal diameters are arranged in a stack.

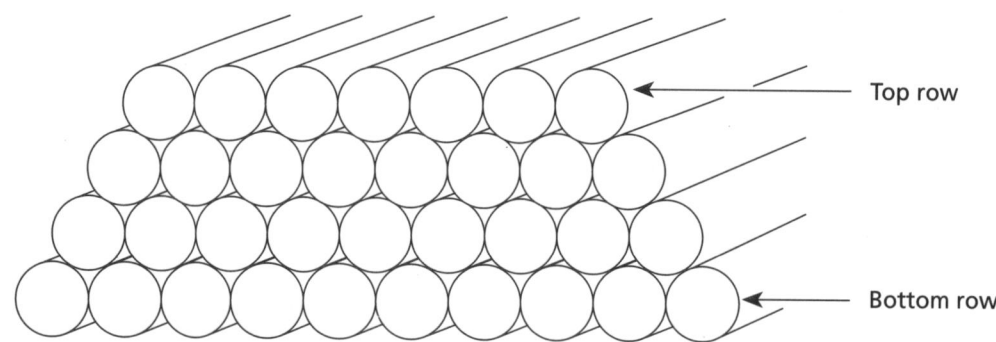

Top row

Bottom row

To find the number of pipes, P, in a stack, the following formula can be used

$$P = \frac{(b+a)(b-a+1)}{2}$$

where b is the number of pipes on the bottom row and a is the number of pipes on the top row.

(a) Use this formula to find the number of pipes in a stack where $b = 40$ and $a = 15$.

.... (1)

(b) In a particular stack, the number of pipes on the bottom row is twice the number on the top row.

Show that in this stack $P = \dfrac{3a^2 + 3a}{2}$ where a is the number of pipes on the top row.

....

....

.... (3)

10

(c) Would it be possible to arrange exactly 975 pipes in the kind of stack described in part (b)?

Justify your answer.

....

....

.... (3)

SEB 1995

3 Freda wants to make a run for her rabbits. She has a roll of netting 22 m long and is going to use it to make three sides of a rectangle. The other side will be part of the garden fence. The length of the side at right angles to the fence is x m. The area inside will be 60 m².

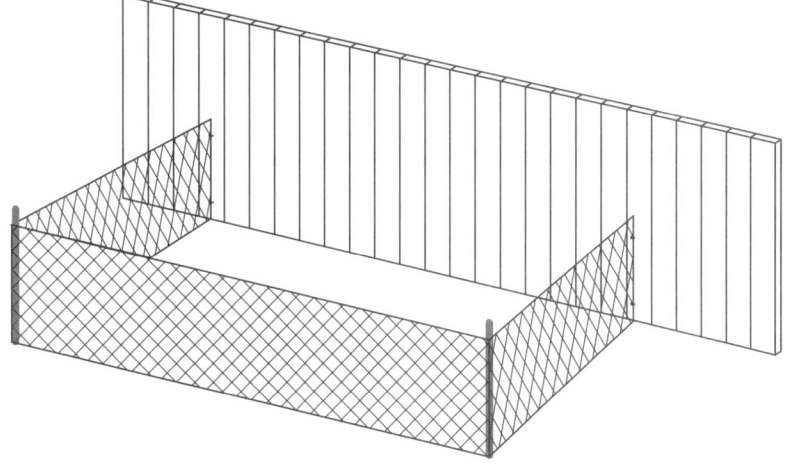

(a) Show that $x^2 - 11x + 30 = 0$.

.... (3)

(b) Solve the equation.

....

....

Answer $x =$ _____ (3)

(c) Describe the size of the run.

.... (2)

2 Algebra

QUESTIONS

4 (a) Simplify the following expression

$$\sqrt{\frac{2a^3b^2 \times 4a^2b^{\frac{1}{2}}}{8a^2b \times 9ab^2}}$$

....

....

Answer _____ (2)

(b) Rearrange this equation $s = \frac{1}{2}at^2$ to give t in terms of s.

....

Answer $t =$ _____ (2)

(c) Simplify the following expression

$$\frac{3x^2 - 2x - 1}{x^2 - 1}$$

....

....

....

....

Answer _____ (2)

5 Mr Brick the builder owns a plot of land, $ABCD$. The dimensions are in metres.

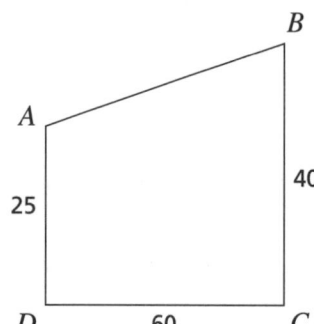

Not to scale

Algebra 2

QUESTIONS

He decides that it is big enough for two houses. He wants to divide it so that the areas of the two parts are equal. The dividing line EF must be parallel to AD and BC. DF = x.

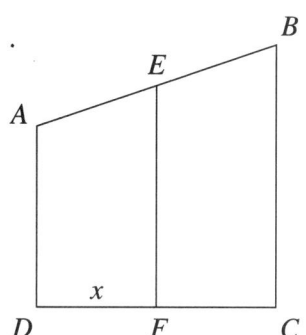

(a) Explain why $EF = 25 + \frac{1}{4}x$.

.... (2)

(b) Show that x satisfies the equation

$$x^2 + 200x - 7800 = 0.$$

....

.... (3)

(c) Solve the equation to find the length of DF. Give your answer to the nearest 0.1 m.

....

....

Answer x = _____ (3)

(d) Explain how you know your answer is about right.

.... (1)

6 (a) Factorise:

  (i) $x^2 - 4$

  .... (1)

  (ii) $2x^2 + 3x - 2$

  ....

  .... (2)

2 Algebra

QUESTIONS

(iii) $6p^2 + 3pq - 2p - q$

....

.... (2)

(b) Simplify $\dfrac{1}{x-2} - \dfrac{4}{x^2-4}$

....

....

....

.... (5)

NICCEA 1995

7 The area of a rectangle is 6 m². If the diagonal is √13 m long what are the dimensions of the rectangle?

....

....

Answer _____ m by _____ m (6)

8 A glass was filled with boiling water and was then left to cool for three hours. The graph below shows the temperature of the water after t minutes.

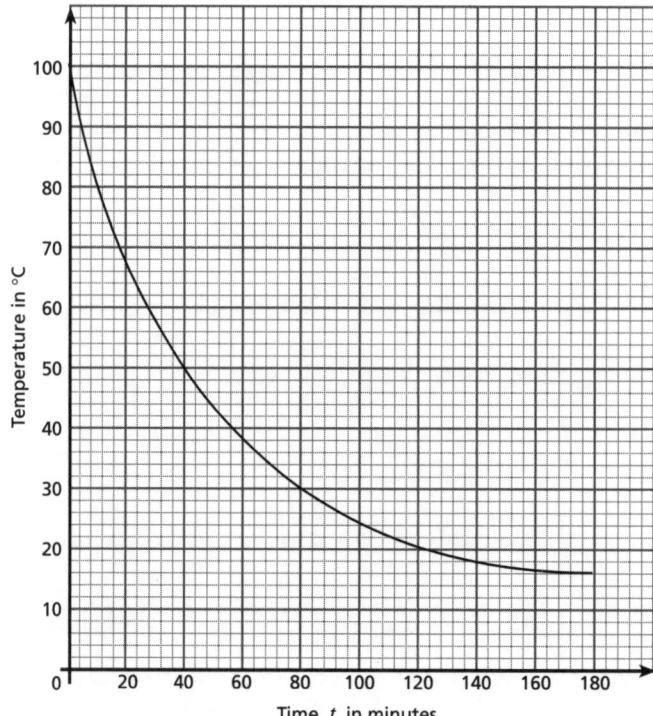

(a) Draw the tangent to the curve at the point where $t = 80$. (1)

(b) Find the gradient of the curve at the point where $t = 80$ and state its units.

....

Answer Gradient = _____

Units _____ (3)

(c) What does the gradient of this graph measure?

.... (1)

MEG 1995

9 These are the stopping distances for cars at various speeds on a dry road:

Speed (*s* miles/hour)	30	50	70
Stopping distance (*d* feet)	75	175	315

There is a formula connecting *d* and *s*.

(a) Show that it is not linear.

....

.... (1)

(b) Show that *d* is not proportional to s^2.

....

.... (1)

(c) The formula is $d = ts + ks^2$. Find the values of *t* and *k*.

....

....

Answer $t =$ _____ $k =$ _____ (5)

2 Algebra

QUESTIONS

10 Write these expressions as simply as possible, using index notation:

(a) $x\sqrt{x}$ (b) $\dfrac{1}{x^2}$ (c) $(x^3 y^2)^2$

....

....

Answer (a) _____ (b) _____ (c) _____ (3)

11

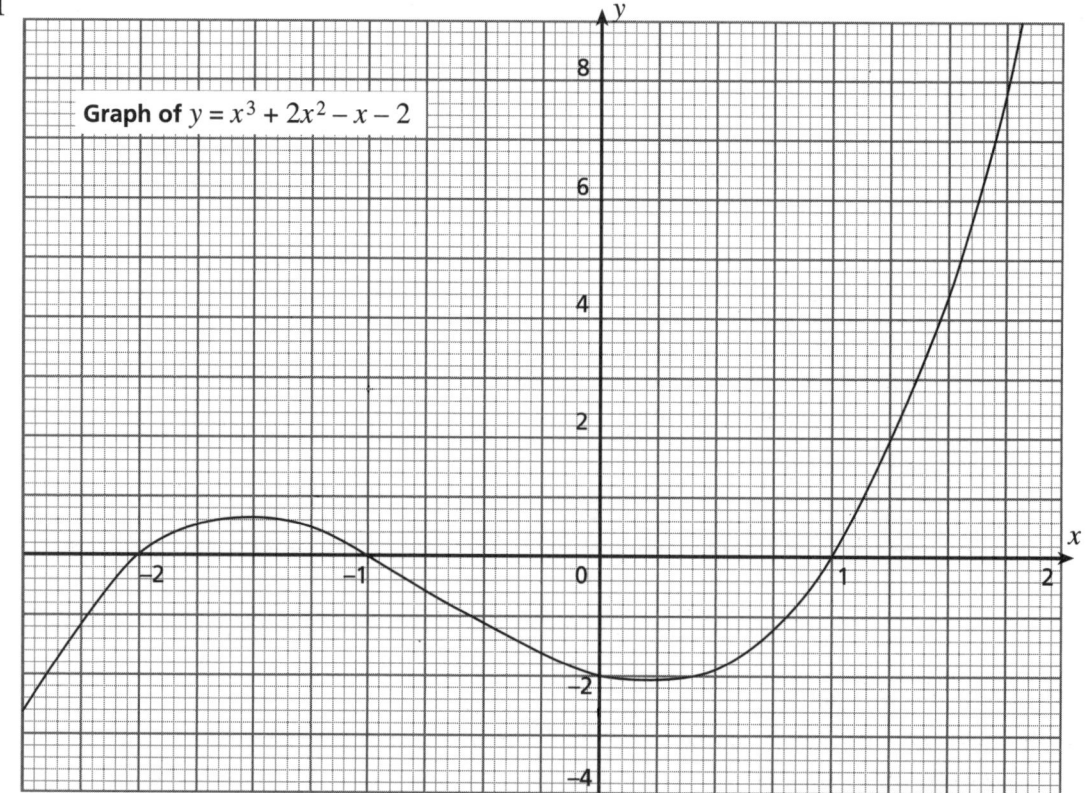

Graph of $y = x^3 + 2x^2 - x - 2$

The diagram above shows the graph of $y = x^3 + 2x^2 - x - 2$.

(a) Use the graph to find the solutions of the equation

$$x^3 + 2x^2 - x - 2 = 0.$$

Answer $x =$ _____ (2)

(b) By drawing the graph of $y = 2x^2$ on the diagram, find the solution of the equation

$$x^3 - x - 2 = 0.$$

....

....

Answer $x =$ _____ (4)

Algebra 2

QUESTIONS

(c) Use the graph to find solutions of the equation

$$x^3 + 2x^2 - x - 1 = 0.$$

....

....

Answer $x =$ _____ (3)

MEG 1995

12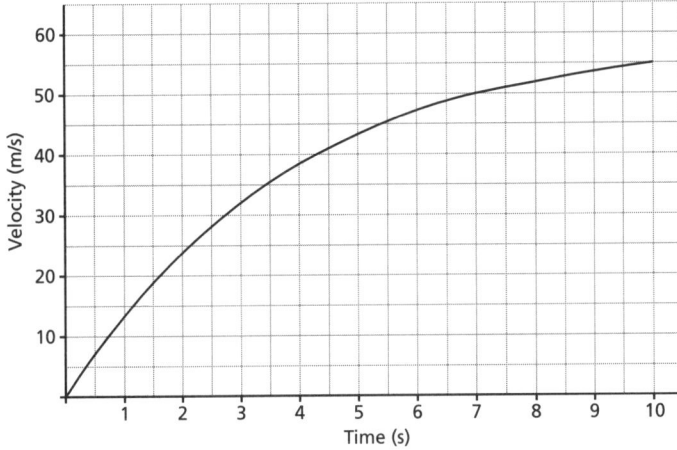

This graph shows the velocity of a sports car starting from rest.

(a) Find the acceleration at time $t = 4$. State the units in your answer.

....

Answer _____ (3)

(b) Estimate how far the car has travelled during the first 10 seconds.
Make your method clear.

....

Answer _____ m (4)

13 The diagram shows the cross section of part of a river bed. *AB* is the water surface.
The units are metres.

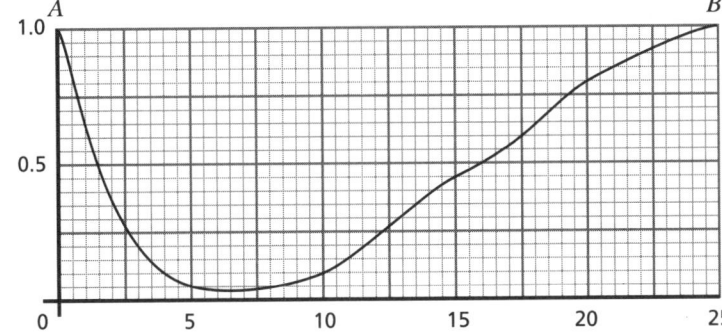

17

2 Algebra

QUESTIONS

Find the area of cross section.

....

....

Answer _____ m² (3)

14 The graph of $y = f(x)$ where $f(x) = \dfrac{x}{x+1}$ is sketched below.

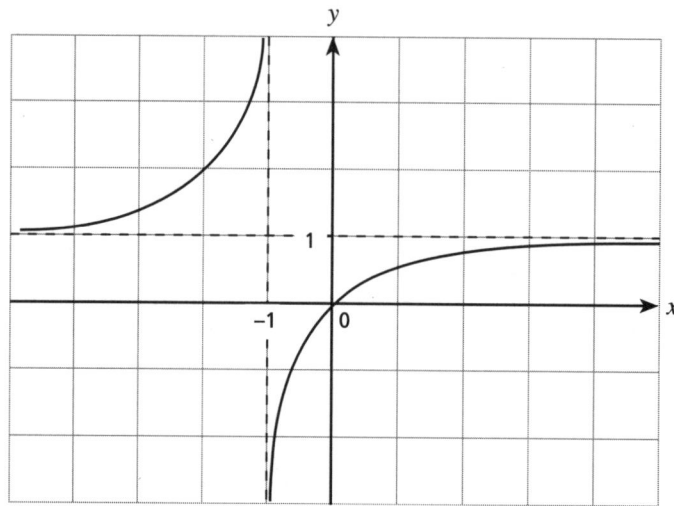

Hence, or otherwise, sketch on the axis below

(a) $y = f(x - 1)$

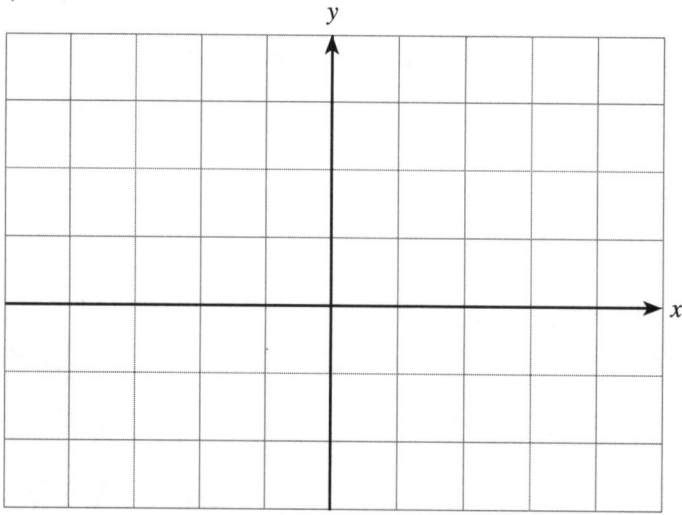

(2)

Algebra 2

QUESTIONS

(b) $y = f(2x)$

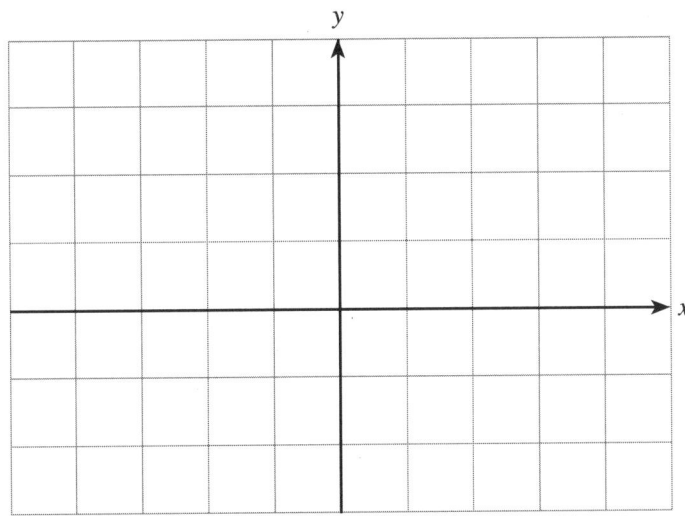

(2)

SEG 1995

15 The sketch shows the graph of the function
$$y = f(x).$$

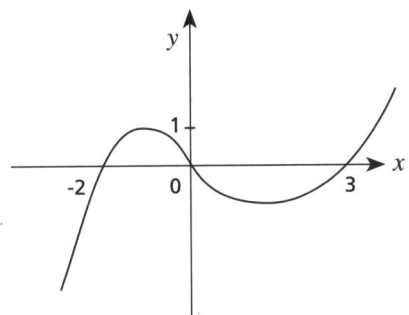

On the diagrams below, sketch the graphs of:

$y = f(x) + 2$

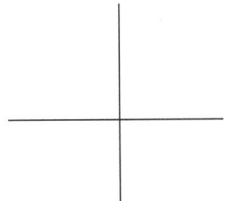

$y = f(x + 2)$

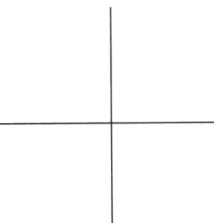

$y = f(x) - 3$

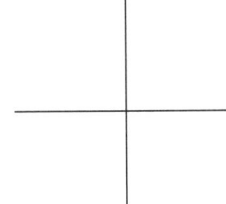

$y = f(x - 3)$

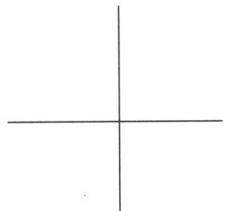

(4)

2 Algebra

QUESTIONS

16 This is part of the graph of $y = x^3 - 3x$.

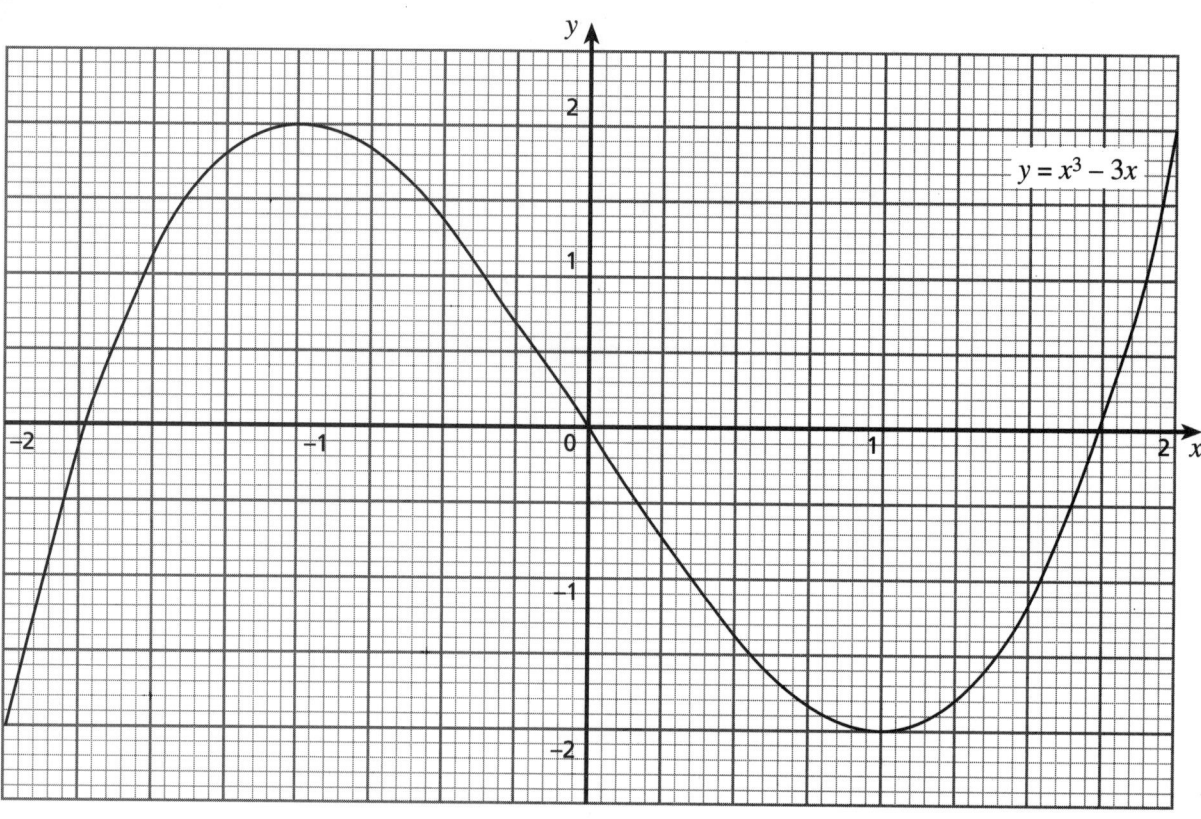

(a) Use the graph to solve the equation

$$x^3 - 3x = 1.$$

....

Answer $x =$ _____ (2)

(b) By drawing a suitable straight line, solve the equation

$$x^3 - 2x = 1.$$

....

Answer $x =$ _____ (3)

17 (a) (i) Show that the equation

$$\frac{1}{x} - \frac{1}{x+2} = \frac{2}{15}$$

can be written in the form

$$x^2 + 2x - 15 = 0.$$

(3)

(ii) Hence solve the equation

$$\frac{1}{x} - \frac{1}{x+2} = \frac{2}{15}.$$

(2)

(b) (i) Express

$$\frac{1}{x} - \frac{1}{x+1}$$

as a single fraction, simplifying your answer as far as possible.

(2)

(ii) Using your answer to (b) (i), write down a positive solution to the equation

$$\frac{1}{x} - \frac{1}{x+1} = \frac{1}{72}.$$

(1)

WJEC 1996

3 Shape and space

REVISION SUMMARY

Solution of problems in more **complicated 2-D and 3-D** situations will be required by some questions in this attainment target. In solid shapes you will need to locate suitable plane sections in order to find the necessary angles and distances.

Example 1:

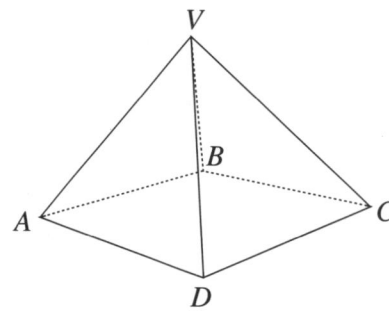

All the edges of this square-based pyramid are length 5 cm.
(a) Find the angle between VC and the base. (Use triangle VAC.)
(b) Find the angle between VCD and the base. (Use the triangle in the plane bisecting CD through V.)

Calculations will also be asked for in triangles which do not contain right angles. Here the **cosine rule** or the **sine rule** can be used.

Example 2: Find the length of QR and the size of the other angles in this triangle.

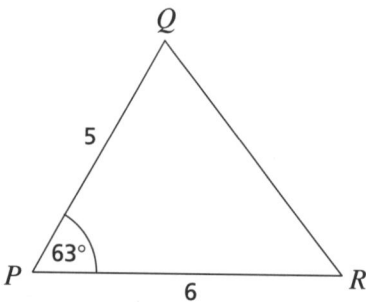

There may also be questions on combining transformations.

Example 3: An object is reflected in $x = 0$ and the result is reflected in $y = 0$.

Describe the single transformation that is equivalent to this.

The last type of question is on vectors, either describing a physical situation, such as a resultant force, or purely in geometry, as in this example.

Example 4: $\mathbf{a} = \begin{pmatrix} 1 \\ 2 \end{pmatrix}$, $\mathbf{b} = \begin{pmatrix} -3 \\ 0 \end{pmatrix}$. Find $2\mathbf{a} - \mathbf{b}$.

If you need to revise this subject more thoroughly, see the relevant topics in the Letts GCSE Mathematics Study Guide or CD-ROM.

Answers to examples:

1: (a) 45°   (b) 54.7°
2: $QR = 5.81$; angle $PRQ = 50.1°$; angle $PQR = 66.9°$
3: Half turn about the origin.
4: $\begin{pmatrix} 5 \\ 4 \end{pmatrix}$

Shape and space 3

QUESTIONS

1 How many spherical balls of radius 1 cm can be made from a large spherical ball of 3 cm radius?

....

....

Answer _____ (2)

2 A lampshade is made by removing the top *VCA* from a hollow cone *VDB* of height 36 cm as shown. The diameter *DB* at the base of the cone is 30 cm and the diameter, *AC*, of the base of the cone removed is 10 cm.

(a) Find the height h of the lampshade.

....

....

....

Answer _____ cm (3)

(b) Find the area of the material needed to cover the lampshade.

....

....

....

Answer _____ cm² (6)

Area of curved surface of a cone = πrl

3 Shape and space

QUESTIONS

3 Brian has a photograph measuring 135 mm by 90 mm. It is enlarged until the shorter side is 110 mm.

(a) How long is the other side?

....

....

Answer _____ mm (2)

The cost of printing a photograph is proportional to its area. The smaller one costs 7p.

(b) How much will the larger one cost?

....

....

....

Answer _____ p (3)

4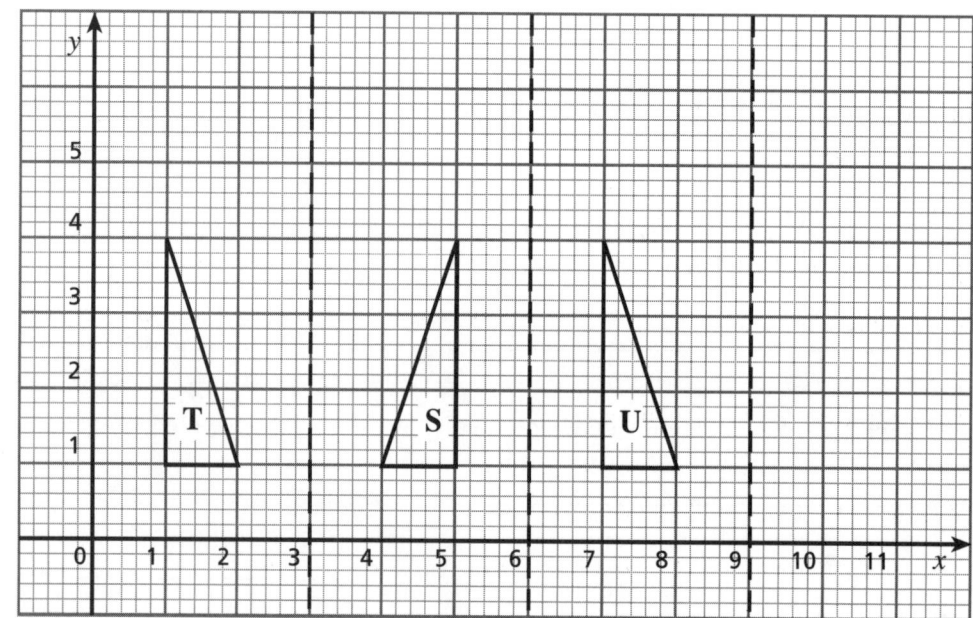

The diagram shows triangles **T**, **S** and **U**.

S is the image of **T** under a reflection in the line $x = 3$. **U** is the image of **S** under reflection in the line $x = 6$.

A reflection in the line $x = 3n$ where n is an integer, is denoted by R_n.

So **S** is the image of **T** under R_1 and **U** is the image of **T** under R_1 followed by R_2.

V is the image of **T** under the successive transformations R_1 followed by R_2 followed by R_3.

(a) Draw **V** on the diagram. (1)

(b) Describe fully the single transformation that will map **T** to **V**.

....

.... (2)

W is the image of **T** under the successive transformations R_1 followed by R_2, followed by R_3 and so on to R_n.

(c) Describe fully the single tranformation that will map **T** to **W**

   (i) when n is even,

   ....

   .... (2)

   (ii) when n is odd.

   ....

   .... (2)

   ULEAC 1995

5 A model power boat can travel at 0.75 m/s in still water. It is released from a point P on the bank of a river which flows at 0.4 m/s. The river is 15 m wide. The boat is aimed continually in a direction perpendicular to the flow of the river, as shown in the diagram.

   (a) By scale drawing or by calculation, find

   (i) the resultant speed of the boat; (2)

   (ii) the direction in which the boat actually travels across the river. (2)

Answers: (i) _____ (ii) _____

3 Shape and space

QUESTIONS

(b) (i) How far downstream from *P* does the boat land on the opposite bank?

.... (2)

(ii) How long does the boat take to cross the river?

.... (2)

NEAB 1995

6 Find the heights of these isosceles triangles.

(a) Triangle ABC with apex A, base BC = 8, D midpoint of BC, angles at B and C each 73°, height AD = ?

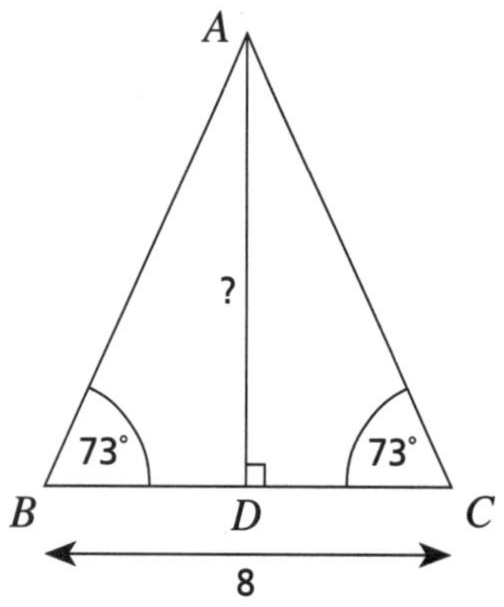

Answer _____ (4)

(b) Triangle PQR with apex P, PQ = PR = 13, base QR = 8, S midpoint of QR, height PS = ?

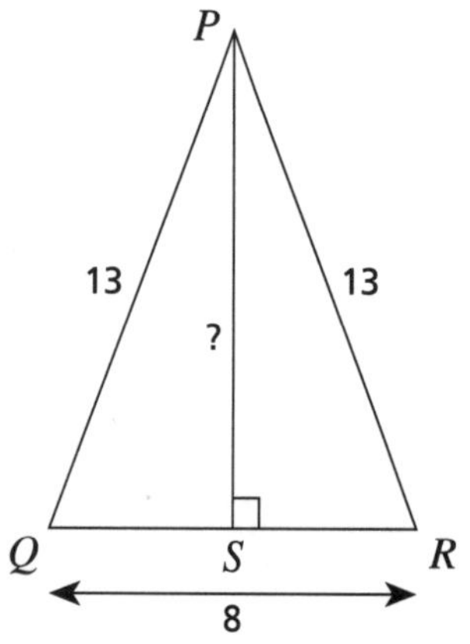

Answer _____ (3)

(c) Triangle with sides 169 and 130, base 169, height = ?

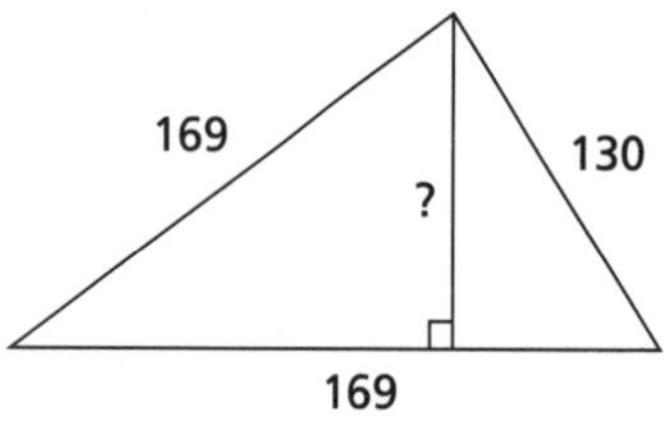

Answer _____ (6)

Shape and space 3

QUESTIONS

7 This is Shirley's garden shed.
It is 2.5 m long.

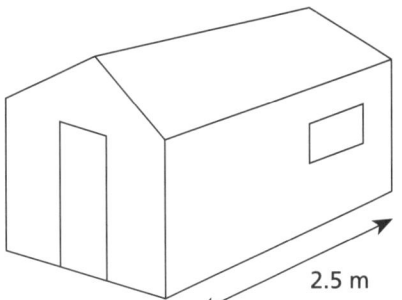

Here are the plan and elevations of the shed:

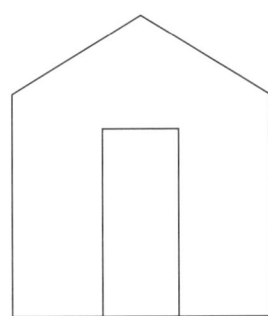 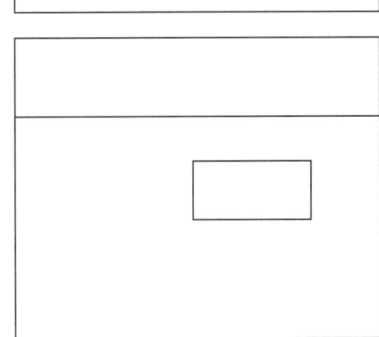

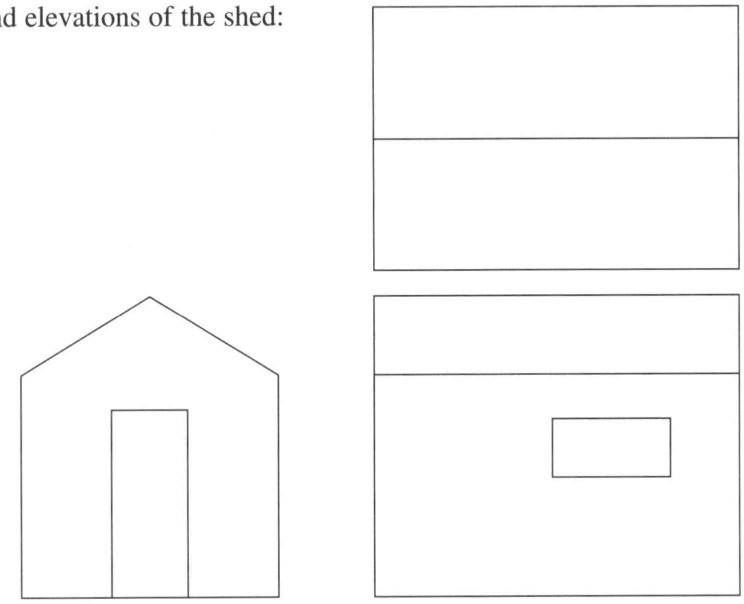

(a) What is the scale of the plan?

Answer _____ (1)

(b) How high is the shed?

....

Answer _____ m (1)

(c) Shirley has a pole 3.25 m long.
She tries to put it in the shed as shown:

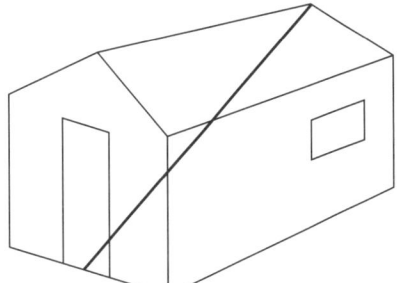

Use calculation to see whether it will fit.

....

.... (3)

3 Shape and space

QUESTIONS

(d) Find the length of the longest pole that will fit into the shed in any position.

....

....

....

Answer _____ m (5)

8 4 cylindrical rods, each of radius 1 cm are packed into a cylindrical container as shown below. (The centres of the rods are at the corners of a square.)

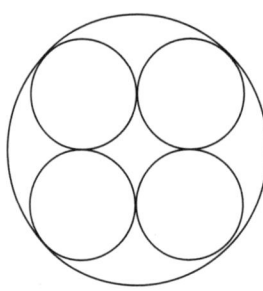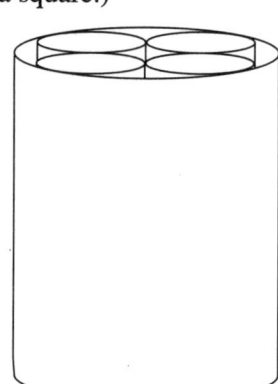

Calculate the radius of the container.

....

....

....

Answer _____ cm (5)

9 The depth of water in the harbour at St Nazaire is given by the formula

$$D = L + K\sin(29.2t)°$$

where $L - K$ is the depth at low tide
$L + K$ is the depth at high tide
t is the time in hours since midnight on 1 July.

(a) At what time is the first high tide on 1 July?

....

Answer _____ (2)

(b) At what time is the first low tide on 1 July?

....

Answer _____ (2)

(c) Is the depth of water in the harbour more or less at midnight on 2 July than at midnight on 1 July? Show how you decided.

....

Answer _____ (2)

(d) Is the tide rising or falling at midnight on 5 July? Show how you decided.

....

Answer _____ (3)

10 Figure 1 shows a road bridge.

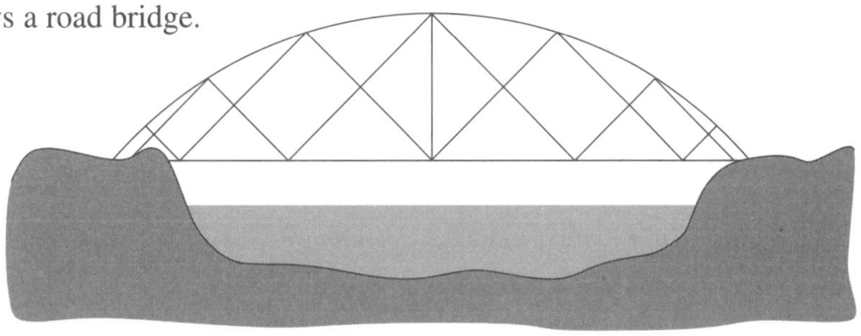

Figure 1

The curved part of the bridge is formed from an arc of a circle, centre O, as shown in Figure 2.

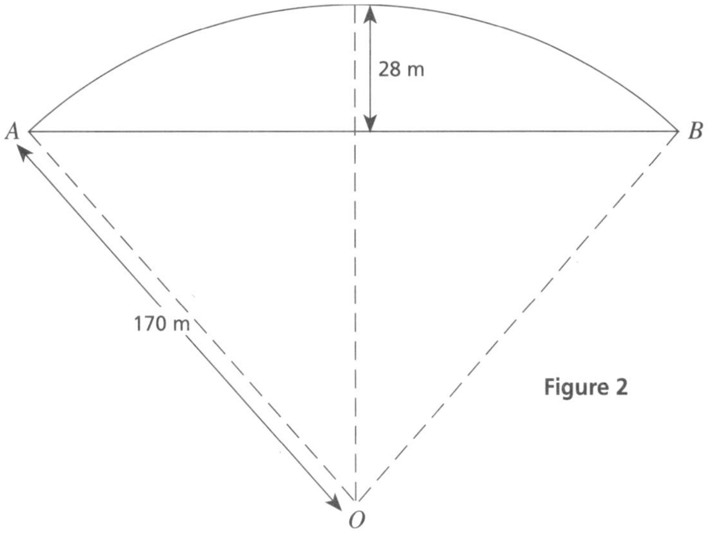

Figure 2

OA and *OB* are radii of length 170 metres.

The height of the middle of the bridge above its ends is 28 metres as shown in Figure 2.

Calculate the horizontal distance, *AB*.

Do not use a scale drawing.

....

.... (4)

SEB 1995

3 Shape and space

QUESTIONS

11 Two people are pulling ropes attached to a box as shown:

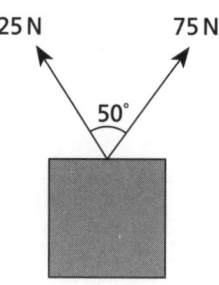

(a) Sketch a vector triangle to show the resultant force.

(2)

(b) Find the size of the resultant force and the angle it makes with the 25 N force.

....

....

Answer _____ N, _____ ° (8)

12 This picture shows a goods van as used on the Welshpool and Llanfair Railway.

This diagram shows one end.
The roof is a circular arc, centre B.
RP = 2.10 m, PQ = 2.33 m.

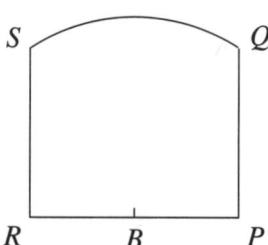

(a) Calculate (i) the length of BQ,

....

Answer _____ m (2)

Shape and space 3

(ii) the angle *BQP*,

....

Answer _____ ° (3)

(iii) the length of the arc *QS*.

....

Answer _____ cm (3)

(b) Calculate the area of the end *RSQP*.

....

....

Answer _____ m² (4)

Penelope has made a model of the van to a scale $\frac{1}{19}$.

(c) (i) How wide is the model?

....

Answer _____ cm (1)

(ii) What is the area of the end of the model?

....

Answer _____ cm² (2)

13 In this diagram *PQRS* is a parallelogram.

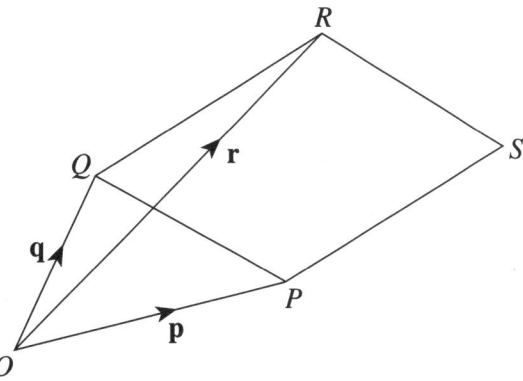

(a) Vector $\overrightarrow{OP} = \mathbf{p} = \begin{pmatrix} 2 \\ 1 \end{pmatrix}$ Vector $\overrightarrow{OQ} = \mathbf{q} = \begin{pmatrix} 1 \\ 3 \end{pmatrix}$

(i) Express vector $\overrightarrow{PQ}$ in terms of **p** and **q**.

Answer $\overrightarrow{PQ}$ = _____ (1)

3 Shape and space

QUESTIONS

(ii) Express vector $\vec{PQ}$ as a column vector.

....

Answer $\vec{PQ}$ = $\begin{pmatrix} \\ \end{pmatrix}$ (1)

(iii) What other vector on the diagram is equal to $\vec{PQ}$?

Answer _____ (1)

Vector $\vec{OR}$ = **r**

(b) (i) Complete the vector equation

$\vec{RQ}$ = $\vec{RO}$ + _____ (1)

(ii) Express vector $\vec{SP}$ in terms of **r** and **q**.

Answer $\vec{SP}$ = _____ (1)

SEG 1995

14 The banks of a river are straight and parallel.

To find the width of the river, two points, *A* and *B*, are chosen 50 m apart.

The angles made with a tree at *C* on the opposite bank are measured as angle *CAB* = 56°, angle *CBA* = 40°.

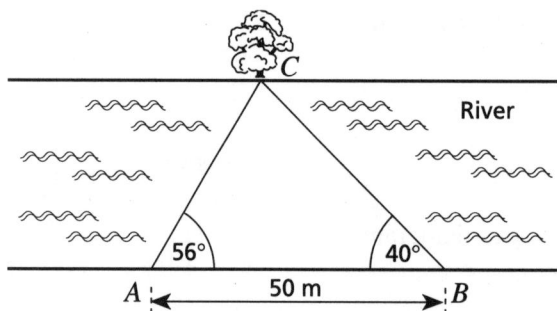

Calculate the width of the river.

....

....

....

....

Answer _____ m (5)

SEG 1995

15 ABCD is the rectangular base of a pyramid with vertex V. V is **not** directly over the centre of the base. The measurements in the diagram are in centimetres.

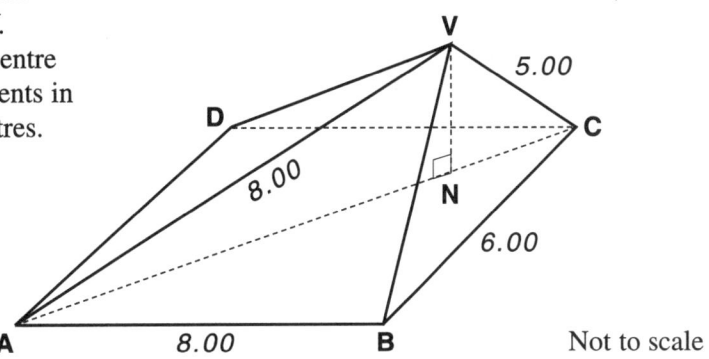

Not to scale

Calculate

(a) AC,

....

....

....

Answer AC = _____ cm

(b) the angle AVC,

....

....

....

Answer angle AVC = _____ °

(c) The height of the pyramid, VN.
Give your answer correct to two decimal places.

....

....

....

.... (8)

Answer VN = _____ cm

MEG 1996

3 Shape and space

QUESTIONS

16 (a) Sketch the graph of $y = \cos x°$ on the given axes.

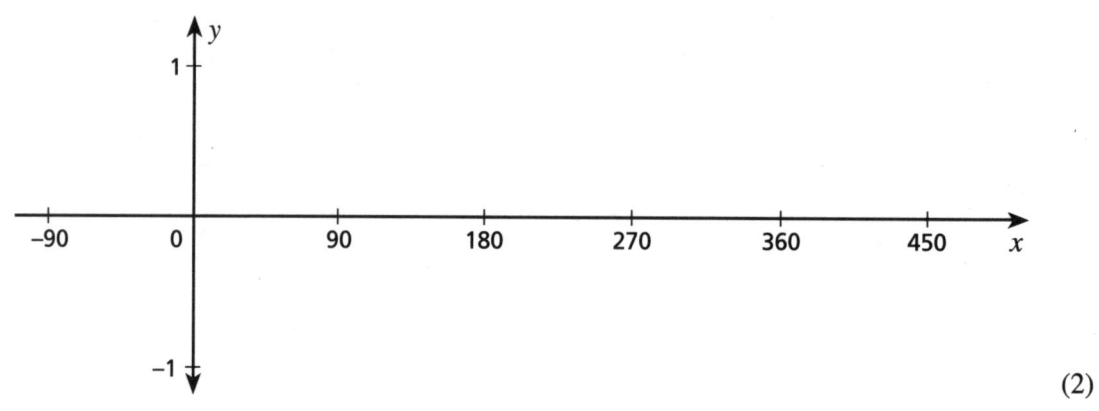

(2)

(b) Use your calculator to find the value of x between 0 and 90 for which $\cos x° = 0.5$.

Answer $x =$ _____ (1)

(c) Using your graph and the answer to part (b), find two more solutions in the range $-90 \leqslant x \leqslant 450$ for which $\cos x° = 0.5$.

....

Answer $x =$ _____ and $x =$ _____ (2)

MEG 1995

Handling data 4

REVISION SUMMARY

There will be questions in this section about **collecting, processing and interpreting data.**
Calculations to find measures of central tendency and spread will be required, such as the mean and standard deviation. It is useful here to have a calculator which has these functions and to learn how to use it. Histograms may be drawn for frequency distributions where the frequency is represented by the area under the histogram, not by the heights of the columns. The axis up the page will be *frequency density*.

Example 1: The table shows the frequency distribution of the heights of 50 girls in a primary school.

(a) Calculate estimates of the mean and standard deviation.
(b) Complete the frequency density column.

Height (x cm)	Frequency	Frequency density
$95 \leq x < 105$	7	
$105 \leq x < 115$	13	
$115 \leq x < 120$	14	
$120 \leq x < 125$	8	
$125 \leq x < 145$	8	

The last topic in this section is **probability**. Many of the situations which you will be asked about will involve conditional probability, where the probabilities are different depending on what happens before the event, such as:

Example 2: The probability that it will rain today is 0.6.
If it rains today, the probability that it will rain tomorrow is 0.4.
If it is fine today, the probability that it will be fine tomorrow is 0.7.
What is the probability that just one of the two days will be wet?

Answers to examples:

1: (a) mean = 116.7, standard deviation = 10.5
   (b) Frequency density: 0.7, 1.3, 2.8, 1.6, 0.4
2: 0.48

If you need to revise this subject more thoroughly, see the relevant topics in the Letts GCSE Mathematics Study Guide or CD-ROM.

4 Handling data

QUESTIONS

1. In a survey 50 people were asked how many hours of television they watched in one week. The histogram shows the results of the survey.

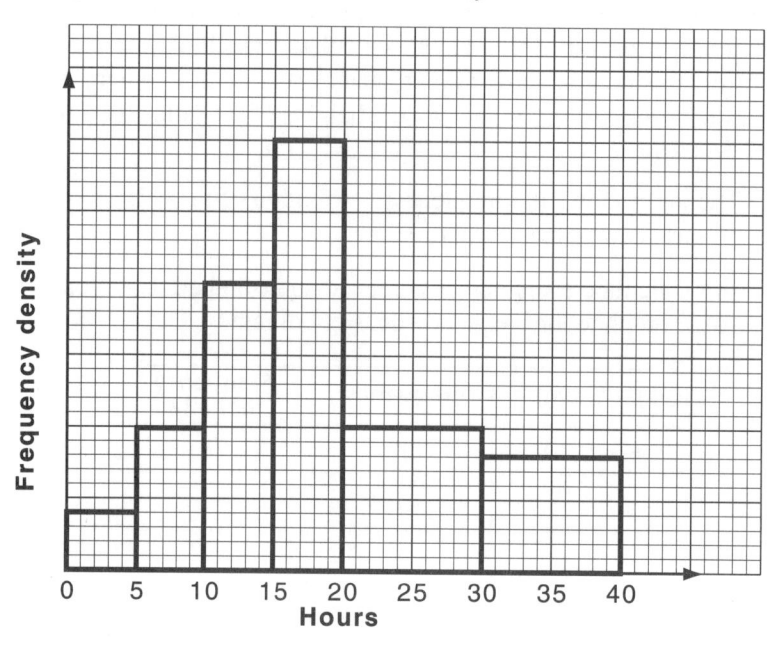

No one watched more than 40 hours of television in one week.

(a) Use the histogram to complete the table of values.

Number of hours	0–	5–	10–	15–	20–	30–40
Frequency	2					

....

.... (3)

(b) The survey was carried out by questioning the first 50 people who went into a shop after 10.00 on a Thursday morning.

   (i) Give one reason why this sample may not be representative of the population.

....

.... (1)

   (ii) Suggest a better way of ensuring that the sample is representative of the population.

....

.... (1)

SEG 1996

Handling data 4

QUESTIONS

2 The West Albion Garden Society has tested two brands of fertilizer for growing marrows. Unfortunately the groupings are different and the results difficult to compare.

BRAND A	
Mass in kg	Frequency
Less than 0.5	1
≥ 0.5 and < 1.0	7
≥ 1.0 and < 2.5	12
≥ 2.5 and < 5.0	10
≥ 5.0 and < 10	3

BRAND B	
Mass in kg	Frequency
Less than 1.0	4
≥ 1.0 and < 2.0	4
≥ 2.0 and < 3.0	6
≥ 3.0 and < 4.0	6
≥ 4.0 and < 5.0	7
≥ 5.0 and < 10	3

(a) Draw the histograms.

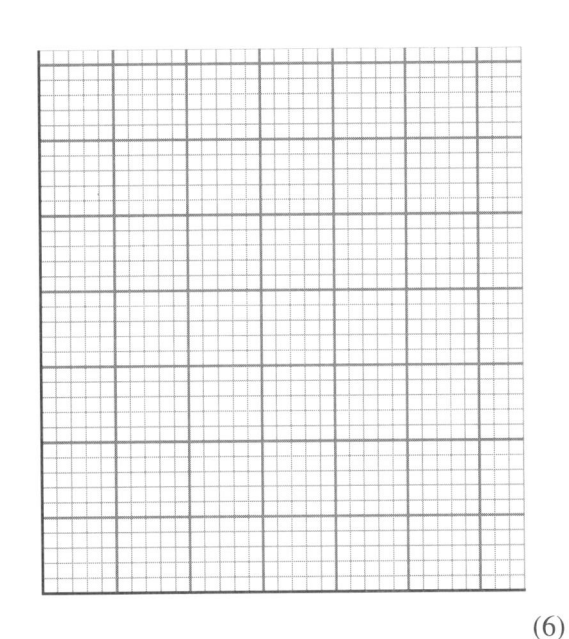

(6)

(b) Calculate estimates of the mean and standard deviation for each brand.

....

....

Answers

A	Mean:	SD:
B	Mean:	SD:

(5)

(c) Compare the results.

.... (2)

4 Handling data

QUESTIONS

3 There are 8 balls in a box. 7 of the balls are yellow and 1 ball is red.
Jean selects balls at random, without replacement, from the box until she obtains the red ball. When she obtains the red ball, then she stops selecting.

By extending the tree diagram shown below, or otherwise, calculate the probability that Jean selects the red ball on one of her first three selections.

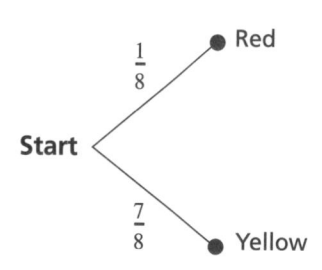

Start
- $\frac{1}{8}$ Red
- $\frac{7}{8}$ Yellow

Answer _____ (3)

ULEAC 1995

4 Sam was making a survey of pupils in his school.

He wanted to find out their opinions on noise pollution by motor bikes.

The size of each year group in the school is shown below.

Year group	Boys	Girls	Total
8	85	65	150
9	72	75	147
10	74	78	152
11	77	72	149
6th Form	93	107	200
			798

Sam took a sample of 80 pupils.

(a) Explain whether or not he should have sampled equal numbers of boys and girls in year 8.

.... (1)

(b) Calculate the number of pupils he should have sampled in year 8.

....

Answer _____ (3)

ULEAC 1995

Handling data 4

QUESTIONS

5 A canteen offers a choice of main course and sweet. For each course one of two choices must be selected.

The tree diagram below shows the choices that a customer can make, and some of the probabilities of those choices.

(a) Complete the tree diagram.

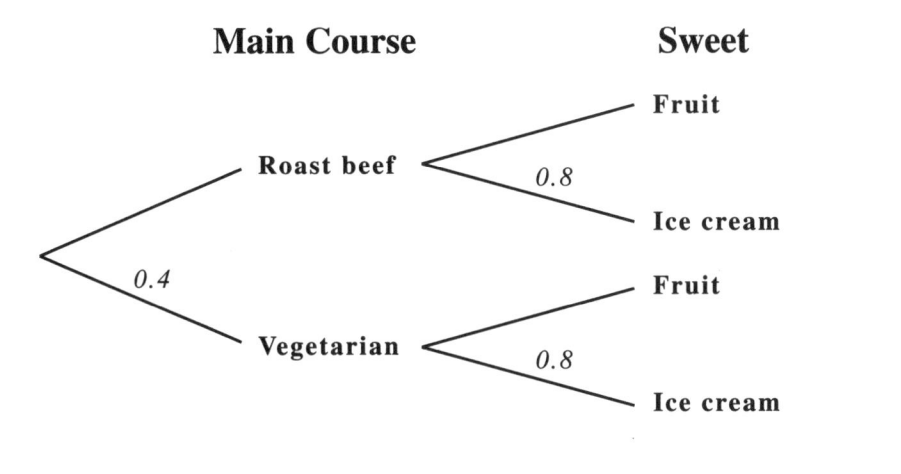

```
         Main Course           Sweet
                              ╱ Fruit
              Roast beef  <
                         0.8
                              ╲ Ice cream
        0.4
                              ╱ Fruit
              Vegetarian  <
                         0.8
                              ╲ Ice cream
```
(1)

(b) Work out the probability that a customer chooses roast beef and ice cream.

....

....

Answer _____ (2)

Experience has shown that the choices are not independent of one another.

If a customer chooses roast beef the probability of choosing fruit is 0.3 but if they choose vegetarian then the probability of choosing fruit is only 0.1.

The probability of choosing vegetarian stays at 0.4.

(c) Show these revised probabilities on the tree diagram below.

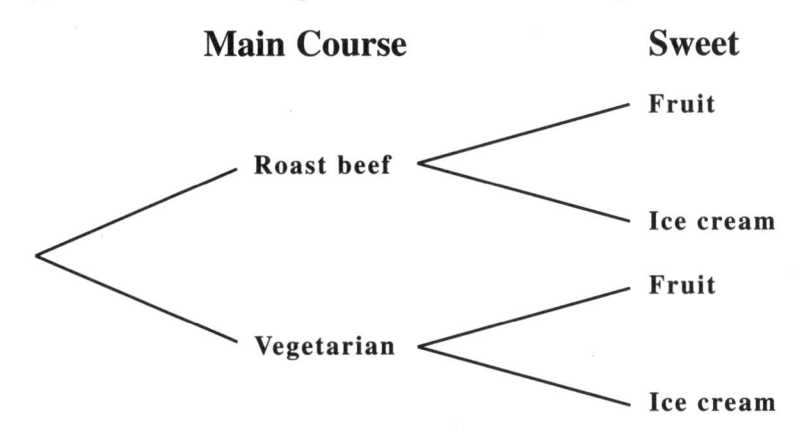

```
         Main Course           Sweet
                              ╱ Fruit
              Roast beef  <
                              ╲ Ice cream

              Vegetarian  <   ╱ Fruit
                              ╲ Ice cream
```
(3)

39

4 Handling data

QUESTIONS

(d) Using your tree diagram from (c), calculate the probability that a customer chooses ice cream for sweet.

....

....

....

....

Answer _____ (3)

SEG 1996

6 The heights of a group of 310 pupils are recorded in the table.

Height	Number of pupils
up to but not including 120 cm	0
120 cm up to but not including 140 cm	80
140 cm up to but not including 150 cm	60
150 cm up to but not including 160 cm	70
160 cm up to but not including 165 cm	40
165 cm up to but not including 180 cm	60
180 cm or more	0

Complete the histogram on the grid on the opposite page.

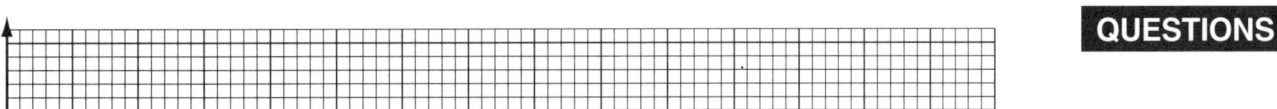

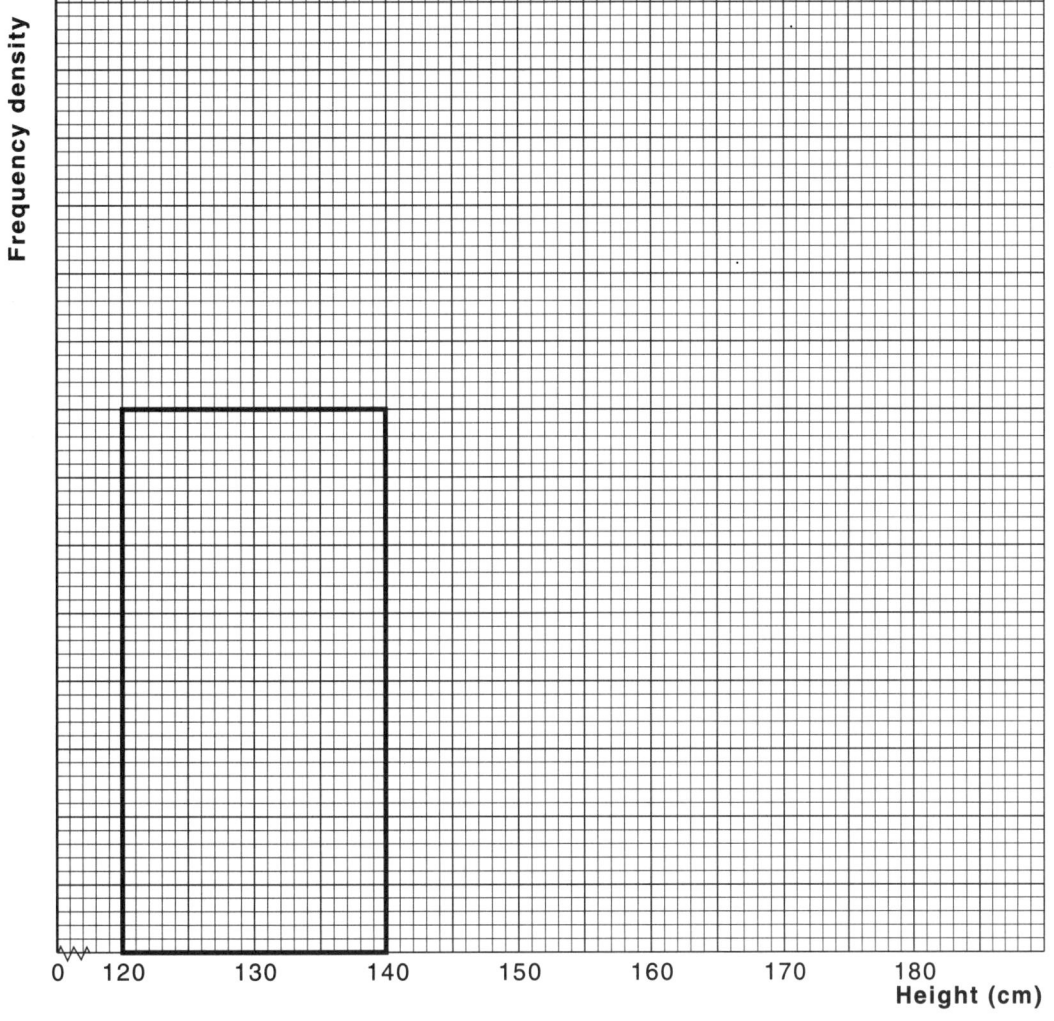

Handling data 4

QUESTIONS

(graph with axes "Frequency density" vs "Height (cm)", showing a rectangle from 120 to 140 on the x-axis)

(4)

ULEAC 1996

4 Handling data

QUESTIONS

7 In the game of tennis a player has two serves.

If the first serve is successful the game continues.

If the first serve is not successful the player serves again. If this second service is successful the game continues.

If both serves are unsuccessful the player has served a "double fault" and loses the point.

Gabriella plays tennis. She is successful with 60% of her first serves and 95% of her second serves.

(a) Calculate the probability that Gabriella serves a double fault.

Answer (a) _____ (3)

If Gabriella is successful with her first serve she has a probability of 0.75 of winning the point.

If she is successful with her second serve she has a probability of 0.5 of winning the point.

(b) Calculate the probability that Gabriella wins the point.

Answer (b) _____ (4)

MEG 1996

Handling data 4

QUESTIONS

8 Malcolm is playing a game with three ordinary dice, faces numbered 1, 2, 3, 4, 5, 6. He throws each in turn. He wins the game if any one shows a six.

(a) (i) Complete the tree diagram.

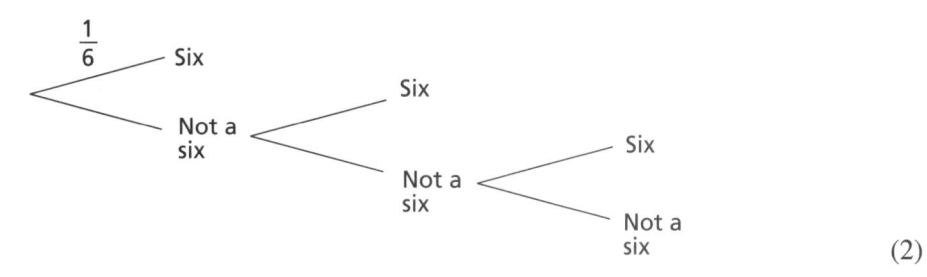

```
        1/6 ─── Six
       /
      ‹          ─── Six
       \        /
        Not a ‹
        six    \       ─── Six
                Not a /
                six  ‹
                      \
                       Not a
                       six
```
(2)

(ii) What is the probability that he wins with the second throw?

....

Answer _____ (2)

(iii) What is the probability that he wins?

....

Answer _____ (3)

Veronica is playing another game with six cards numbered 1, 2, 3, 4, 5, 6. She takes a card at random and does not replace it. If it is a six she wins. If not, she draws another card, again not replacing it. If it is a six she wins. If not, a third card is drawn. If it is a six she wins.

(b) (i) Complete the tree diagram.

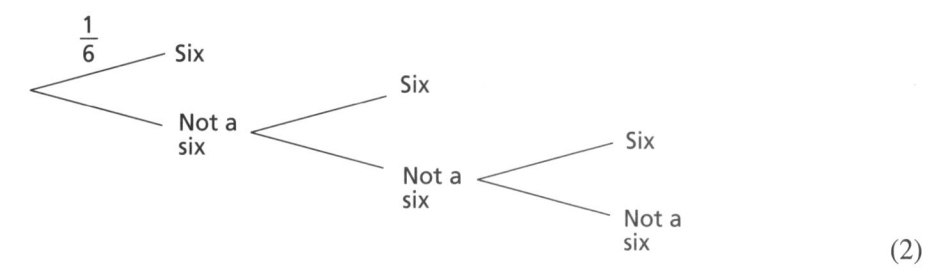

```
        1/6 ─── Six
       /
      ‹          ─── Six
       \        /
        Not a ‹
        six    \       ─── Six
                Not a /
                six  ‹
                      \
                       Not a
                       six
```
(2)

(ii) What is the probability that she wins with the second draw?

....

Answer _____ (2)

(iii) What is the probability that she wins?

....

Answer _____ (3)

(iv) Explain how you could have found the answer to (iii) another way.

.... (1)

4 Handling data

QUESTIONS

9 Ten boys sat a test which was marked out of 50.
Their marks were 28, 42, 35, 17, 49, 12, 48, 38, 24 and 27.

(a) Calculate

(i) the mean of the marks,

.... (2)

(ii) the standard deviation of the marks.

.... (2)

Ten girls sat the same test.
Their marks had a mean of 30 and a standard deviation of 6.5.

(b) Compare the performances of the boys and girls.

.... (2)

NEAB 1995

10 Students finishing a word-processing course had their speeds measured in characters per minute (ch/min) with the following results.

Speed (in ch/min)	Number of students
100 —	20
300 —	34
350 —	40
400 —	32
450 —	28
500 —	12
600 and over	0

Using these axes, draw a histogram to display these data (4)

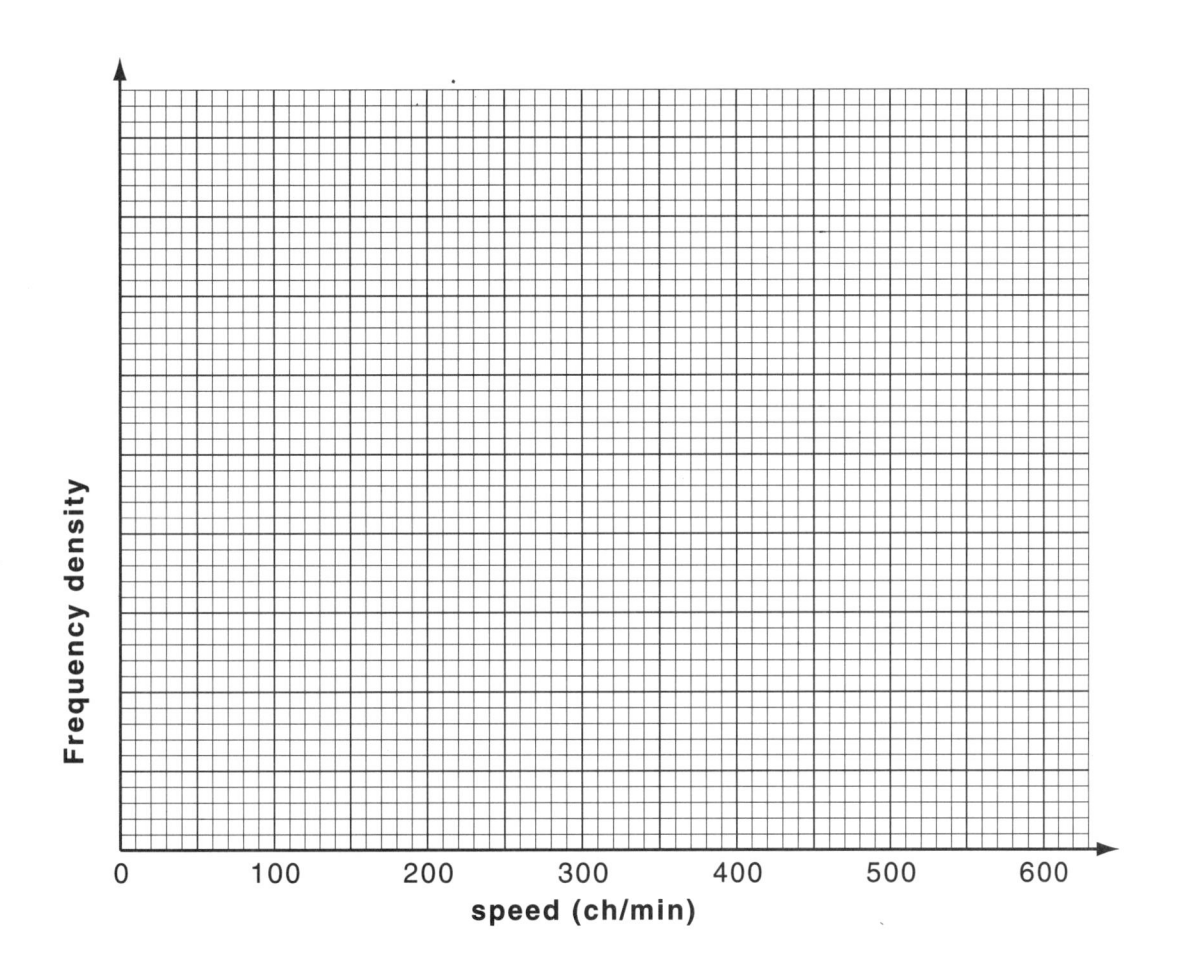

Frequency density (y-axis) vs **speed (ch/min)** (x-axis, 0 to 600)

MEG 1996

11 How many times must you toss a fair coin for the probability of getting at least one head to be more than 0.95?

....

....

Answer _____ (5)

4 Handling data

QUESTIONS

12 The histogram below gives information about the ages of the teachers at a school on 1st September last year.

(a) Use the information in the histogram to complete the frequency table below.

Age (*A*) years	Frequency
22 ≤ A < 24	
24 ≤ A < 27	
27 ≤ A < 30	
30 ≤ A < 35	16
35 ≤ A < 40	19
40 ≤ A < 50	
50 ≤ A < 65	27

(4)

(b) Use the information in the frequency table to complete the histogram. (2)

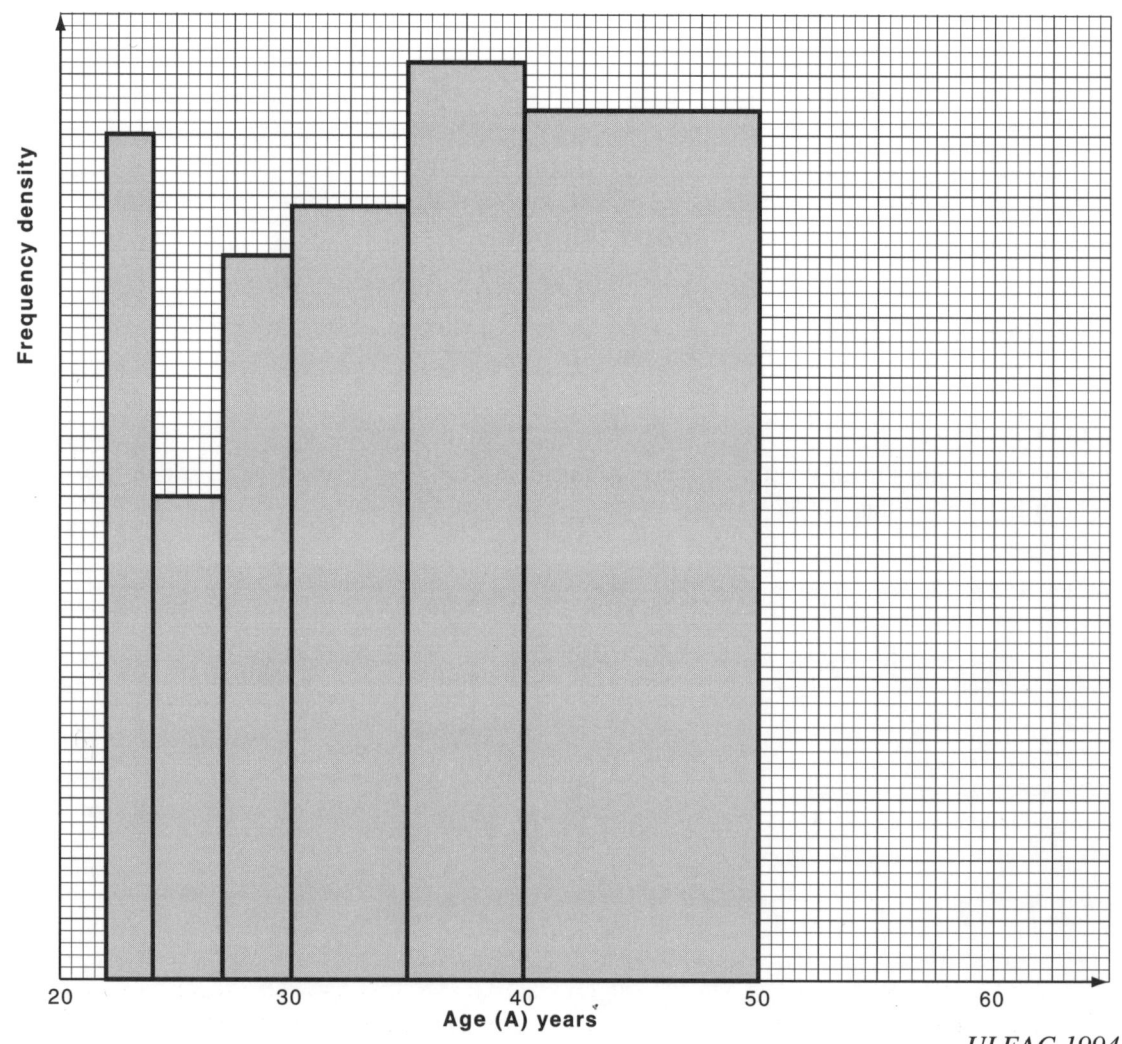

ULEAC 1994

Handling data 4

QUESTIONS

13 Ceri is training for a swimming competition. During a training session, she swims 50 lengths of a swimming pool and her trainer records the time she takes to complete each length. A summary of the times, in seconds, is recorded in the grouped frequency distribution below.

Time t seconds	Frequency f	Frequency density
$85 \leq t < 90$	5	
$90 \leq t < 95$	9	
$95 \leq t < 105$	21	
$105 \leq t < 115$	11	
$115 \leq t \leq 120$	4	

(a) Complete the frequency density column. (1)

(b) On the graph paper below, draw a histogram of the distribution of the times taken by Ceri to swim a length of the pool.

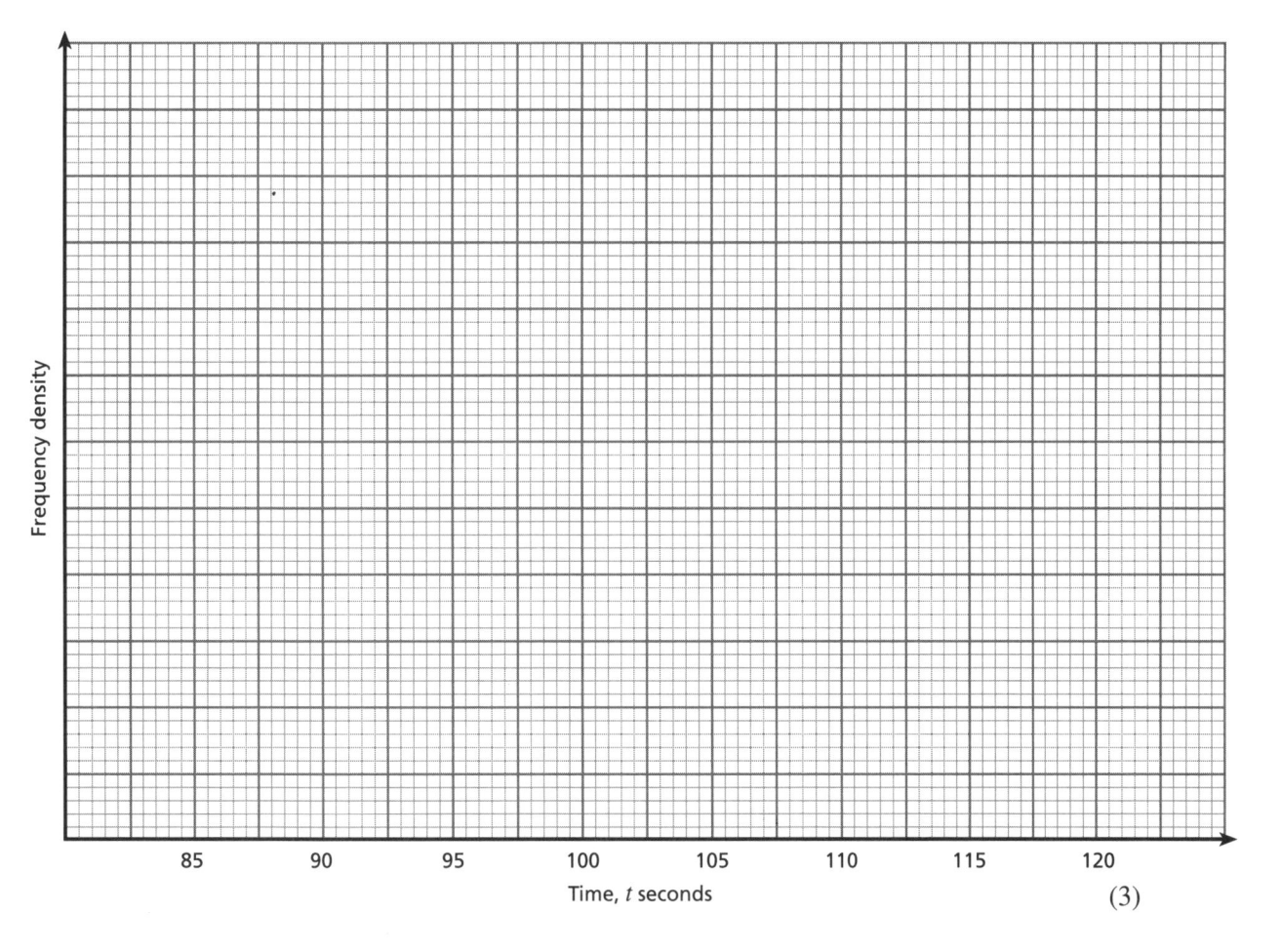

[Graph paper with Frequency density on the y-axis and Time, t seconds on the x-axis, marked from 85 to 120.]

(3)

(c) The times, in seconds, that Ceri took to complete the first 10 lengths were 93, 90, 87, 85, 86, 86, 92, 94, 90, and 92. The mean time for these ten lengths is 89.5 seconds. Find the standard deviation of the times, in seconds, of the first ten lengths, giving your answer correct to one decimal place.

4 Handling data

QUESTIONS

....

.... (2)

(d) Use your histogram to estimate the proportion of lengths, in the whole training session, which took longer than 110 seconds.

....

.... (2)

WJEC 1995

14 The committee of St Minnack & Porthcumo Youth Club consists of 3 boys and 5 girls. At the AGM. the secretary and the treasurer are chosen at random from the committee members. The secretary is chosen first.

(a) What is the probability that one particular boy, Darren, will be chosen as secretary?

....

.... (1)

One of the rules of the Club is that the secretary and the treasurer must be of different sexes. (For example, if a boy is chosen as secretary, then the treasurer is chosen at random from the girls.)

(b) Before either the secretary or the treasurer is chosen, what is the probability that one particular girl, Tamarin, will be chosen as treasurer?

....

.... (2)

(c) Bryn and his sister Gwyneth are two members of the committee.

   (i) Find the probability that Bryn will be chosen as secretary and Gwyneth as treasurer.

....

.... (1)

   (ii) Find the probability that one of them will be chosen as secretary and the other as treasurer.

....

.... (3)

MEG 1996

Answers

1 NUMBER

Question	Answer	Mark
1 (a)	$22 \sin 70° = 20.67$, $28 \sin 48° = 20.81$	2+1
	Perpendicular distance between longest sides is nearly the same at each end.	1
	Longest sides are nearly parallel, so quadrilateral is roughly a trapezium.	1

Examiner's tip The first part of this question requires you to use knowledge from a different attainment target but this is to enable you to tackle the next part. If you did not spot how to do this, come back to it again after practice in a later section.

(b)	Area of largest possible trapezium must be found using upper bounds of lengths.	1
	Maximum area $= \frac{1}{2} \times 21.5 \times (32.5 + 58.5)$	1
	$= 978.25$	1
	Yes, this is less than 1000.	1

Examiner's tip This could have been treated in a more complicated way by using the maximum possible distance between the 'parallel' sides, i.e. $28.5 \sin 48.5°$, which is 21.3 and $22.5 \sin 70.5°$, which is 21.2, both smaller than 21.5 which had been taken as the upper bound of 21. The result would clearly have been smaller.

In some problems it may be necessary to take a lower bound, even though the maximum value of the expression is required, for example where division is involved.

2 (a)	(i)	815	(ii)	805	1+1
(b)	(i)	2.935	(ii)	2.925	1+1
(c)	(i)	$815 \div 2.925$			1
		$= 278.6324...$			1
	(ii)	$805 \div 2.935$			1
		$= 274.2759...$			1
(d)		300			1

Examiner's tip To find the upper bound in part (c), divide the largest by the smallest and vice versa for the lower bound. The answer to part (d) is one significant figure because to two significant figures the upper and lower bounds are different (280, 270).

3 (a)	For example, $\sqrt{20}$ or $\sqrt[3]{70}$	1
(b)	As N is rational, let $N = \frac{p}{q}$, where p and q are integers.	1
	Reciprocal of $N = \frac{q}{p}$, which is rational	1

Answers to Unit 1

Question	Answer	Mark

> **Examiner's tip** In part (a), any irrational between the limits will be right. The proof in part (b) depends on the definition of a rational number, that is it can be expressed as an integer divided by an integer.

4 Maximum average speed $= \dfrac{400.5}{49.35}$ **2**

$= 8.1155…$ or 8.11 **1**

> **Examiner's tip** This is an example where the upper bound of the speed is obtained using the upper bound of the distance with the lower bound of the time. It is not sensible to round up since this would be above the upper bound.

5 (a)   For example, 1, 8, 27, 64, etc.   **1**

    (b)   For example, 2, 3, 4, 5, etc.   **1**

> **Examiner's tip** An answer to part (a) must be a cube number and to part (b) must be any whole number other than a cube number, since index $\tfrac{1}{3}$ means the cube root.

6 (a)   For example, 1.21 or $1\tfrac{21}{100}$ **1**

    (b)   For example, $\sqrt{1.5}$ or $\sqrt{\tfrac{3}{2}}$ **1**

> **Examiner's tip** You may have thought of different answers. They will be right so long as they fall between the limits and are rational/irrational. In part (b) it can help to square the limits (1.44, 1.5625) then choose a number between these. Its square root may be irrational – check. Of course, square roots are not the only irrational numbers.

7 (a)   For example, $\sqrt{40}, \sqrt{60}, \sqrt[3]{250}$, etc.   **1**

    (b)   Let $\quad N = 3.8\dot{4}\dot{}\quad$ i.e. $\quad 3.848\,484…$ **1**

                 $100N = 384.8\dot{4}\dot{}\quad$ i.e. $\quad 384.848\,484…$ **1**

         subtract: $\quad 99N = 381,\ N = \tfrac{381}{99},\ 3\tfrac{28}{33}$ **1+1**

    (c) (i) $\sqrt{2} \times 2\sqrt{3} + \sqrt{6} = 3\sqrt{6}$ Irrational   **1+1**

       (ii) $(3\sqrt{6})^2 = 54$ Rational   **1+1**

      (iii) $\dfrac{2\sqrt{3} \times \sqrt{6}}{\sqrt{2}} = \dfrac{2 \times \sqrt{3} \times \sqrt{2} \times \sqrt{3}}{\sqrt{2}} = 6$ Rational   **1+1**

Answers to Unit 1

Question	Answer	Mark

Examiner's tip It is useful to remember results such as $\sqrt{6} = \sqrt{2 \times 3} = \sqrt{2} \times \sqrt{3}$ to help to simplify expressions.

---

8 (a) $2 \times 8.1 + 2 \times 6.1 = 28.4$ — 1
(or $2 \times 7.9 + 2 \times 5.9 = 27.6$)
Error = 0.4   — 1

(b) Error in $P = 2(l + a + w + b) - 2(l + w)$ — 1
$= 2a + 2b$ — 1

Examiner's tip Notice that the answer required in each part is the maximum error not the maximum value.

---

9 (a) $3.142 = \dfrac{3142}{1000}$ which is rational   — 1

(b) $1.\dot{6} = 1\tfrac{2}{3}$ which is rational   — 1

(c) $\left(\sqrt{3}\right)^3 = 3\sqrt{3}$ which is irrational   — 2

(d) $(1 + \sqrt{3})(1 - \sqrt{3}) = 1 + \sqrt{3} - \sqrt{3} - 3$ — 1
$= -2$ which is rational   — 1

(e) $\dfrac{(1 + \sqrt{3})}{(1 - \sqrt{3})} = \dfrac{(1 + \sqrt{3})(1 + \sqrt{3})}{(1 - \sqrt{3})(1 + \sqrt{3})} = \dfrac{1 + 2\sqrt{3} + 3}{-2}$ — 2

$= -2 - \sqrt{3}$ which is irrational   — 1

Examiner's tip To show that a number is rational it is necessary to show that it can be written as a fraction using whole numbers. In this case an approach to part (e) was suggested by the work in part (d).

---

10 (a) 3.75 hours   — 1
195 miles,   205 miles   — 1+1

(b) Upper bound $= \dfrac{205}{3.25}$ — 1
$= 63.1$ — 1
Lower bound $= \dfrac{195}{3.75}$ — 1
$= 52$ — 1

Examiner's tip It is not asked here, but using measurements taken to this accuracy, it is not possible to state the speed as the bounds are different to one significant figure.

Answers to Unit 2

2 ALGEBRA

Question	Answer	Mark
1 (a)	Next term will be the mean of the previous two terms.	1
(b)	Next three terms are $1\frac{11}{16}$, $1\frac{21}{32}$, $1\frac{43}{64}$, or on the calculator 1.6875, 1.65625, 1.67185	1
	Two more terms: 1.6640625, 1.66795625	1+1
	Limit appears to be $1\frac{2}{3}$.	1

Examiner's tip You may prefer to use the differences between successive terms, $^+1$, $^-\frac{1}{2}$, $^+\frac{1}{4}$, $^-\frac{1}{8}$, etc.

2 (a)	$P = \frac{(40+15)(40-15+1)}{2} = 715$	1
(b)	$b = 2a$	1
	$P = \frac{(2a+a)(2a-a+1)}{2}$	1
	$= \frac{3a(a+1)}{2} = \frac{3a^2+3a}{2}$	1
(c)	$\frac{3a^2+3a}{2} = 975$	
	$3a^2 + 3a = 1950$	
	$a^2 + a - 650 = 0$	1
	$(a + 26)(a - 25) = 0$	1
	$a = 25, b = 50$	1
	Therefore possible	

Examiner's tip In part (b) it is important to show the intermediate steps as the result is given in the question. You may be able to 'spot' the solution in part (c). Notice that the solution $a = ^-26$ is not possible.

3 (a)	The lengths of the three sides are x, x and $22 - 2x$, since the total length of netting is 22 m.	
	Area = $x(22 - 2x) = 60$	1
	$22x - 2x^2 = 60$ (expanding brackets)	
	$11x - x^2 = 30$ (dividing by 2)	1
	$-x^2 + 11x - 30 = 0$ (subtracting 30 from each side)	
	$x^2 - 11x + 30 = 0$ (multiplying each side by $^-1$)	1
(b)	$(x - 5)(x - 6) = 0$	1
	$x - 5 = 0$ or $x - 6 = 0$	1
	$x = 5$ or 6	1

Answers to Unit 2

Question	Answer	Mark

Examiner's tip Since the left-hand side of this equation did factorize, this is the easiest way to solve it. However, the same result would have been achieved by using the quadratic formula or completing the square.

(c) If $x = 5$ the run measures 5 by 12 — 1
If $x = 6$ the run measures 6 by 10 — 1

Examiner's tip Both solutions work in this practical problem. This is not always the case.

4 (a) $\sqrt{\dfrac{a^2 b^{-\frac{1}{2}}}{9}}$ — 1

$\dfrac{a}{3b^{\frac{1}{4}}}$ or $\dfrac{a}{3\sqrt[4]{b}}$ or $\dfrac{1}{3}ab^{-\frac{1}{4}}$ — 1

(b) $t^2 = \dfrac{2s}{a}$ — 1

$t = \sqrt{\dfrac{2s}{a}}$ — 1

(c) $\dfrac{(3x+1)(x-1)}{(x+1)(x-1)}$ — 1

$= \dfrac{(3x+1)}{(x+1)}$ — 1

Examiner's tip Cancel terms first in part (a). Don't forget the factors of x^2-1 in part (c).

5 (a)

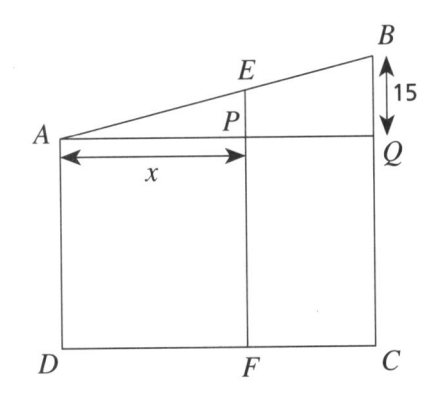

APE and *AQB* are similar triangles so

Answers to Unit 2

Question	Answer		Mark
	$\dfrac{PE}{QB} = \dfrac{AP}{AQ}$	(ratios of corresponding sides)	1
	$PE = x \times 15 \div 60 = \tfrac{1}{4}x$	(substituting)	
	$EF = FP + PE = 25 + \tfrac{1}{4}x$		1
(b)	Area of $AEFD = \tfrac{1}{2}x(AD + EF) = \tfrac{1}{2}x(25 + 25 + \tfrac{1}{4}x)$		1
	Area of $AEFD = \tfrac{1}{2}$ area $ABCD = \tfrac{1}{4} \times 60 \times (25 + 40)$		1
	$25x + \tfrac{1}{8}x^2 = 975$	(simplifying and putting areas equal)	1
	$x^2 + 200x - 7800 = 0$	(multiply by 8 and rearrange)	
(c)	$x = 30$	$x^2 + 200x - 7800 = -900$	
	35	425	1
	33	-111	
	33.5	22.25	
	33.4	-4.44	1
	33.4 is closer		1

> **Examiner's tip** As an alternative, if you know the method, you could use the quadratic formula or 'completing the square'. This quadratic expression did not factorize and there was a clue to this in the question – the answer was asked to the nearest 0.1 m.

(d)	It is just to the right of halfway and DF will be wider than FC since AD is shorter than BC.		1

6 (a)	(i)	$(x + 2)(x - 2)$		1
	(ii)	$(2x - 1)(x + 2)$		2
	(iii)	$(3p - 1)(2p + q)$		2
(b)		$\dfrac{x+2}{(x-2)(x+2)} - \dfrac{4}{(x-2)(x+2)}$		2
		$= \dfrac{x+2-4}{(x-2)(x+2)}$		1
		$= \dfrac{x-2}{(x-2)(x+2)}$		1
		$= \dfrac{1}{x+2}$		1

> **Examiner's tip** Part (a)(i) is a strong hint for part (b). This is the simplest common denominator for the fractions. Make sure you write down each step clearly.

Answers to Unit 2

Question	Answer	Mark
7	Let the lengths of the sides of the rectangle be x and y.	
	$xy = 6$ (area of rectangle)	1
	$\sqrt{x^2 + y^2} = \sqrt{13}$ or $x^2 + y^2 = 13$ (using Pythagoras)	1
	$x^2 + \dfrac{36}{x^2} = 13$ (substituting for y from first equation)	1
	$x^4 - 13x^2 + 36 = 0$ (multiplying each side by x^2 and rearranging)	1
	$(x^2 - 9)(x^2 - 4) = 0$ (factorizing)	1
	$x^2 = 9$ or 4, $x = 3$ or 2	1
	Rectangle is 3m by 2m or 2m by 3m.	

Examiner's tip Although it looks as though this is an equation in x^4 it is only a quadratic in x^2, from the practical point of view. Notice that it is not necessary to consider the negative solutions since the problem was about actual lengths.

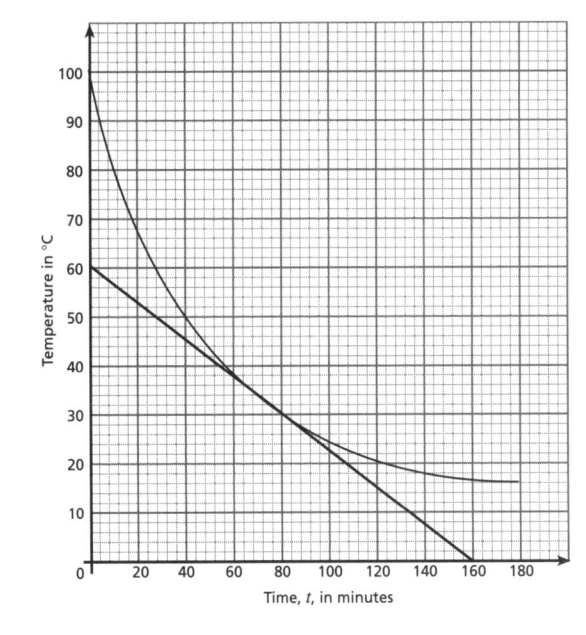

8 (a)	[graph of temperature in °C vs time t in minutes, showing cooling curve and tangent line]	1
(b)	$-\dfrac{60}{160} = -0.375$	2
	°C/minute	1
(c)	Rate of cooling	1

Examiner's tip You will lose a mark in part (b) if you omit the negative sign.

9 (a)	If it were linear the increases would be in proportion: Speed goes up in steps of 20 but distance goes up 100 then 140.	1

Answers to Unit 2

Question	Answer	Mark
(b)	If $d \propto s^2$, then $\left(\dfrac{30}{50}\right)^2 (= 0.36)$ should equal $\left(\dfrac{75}{175}\right) (= 0.42...)$	1
(c)	$75 = 30t + 900k$	
	$175 = 50t + 2500k$	1
	$375 = 150t + 4500k$ (multiplying first by 5)	1
	$525 = 150t + 7500k$ (multiplying second by 3)	1
	$150 = 3000k$ (subtracting)	1
	$k = 0.05$	1
	$t = (75 - 900 \times 0.05) \div 30 = 1$	1

Examiner's tip It is also possible to solve a problem like this by drawing the graph of d against s^2 and finding the gradient and intercept.

10 (a)	$x^{3/2}$	1
(b)	x^{-2}	1
(c)	$x^6 y^4$	1

Examiner's tip Notice in part (c) that the answer is not $x^5 y^4$ achieved by adding indices. It is perhaps clearer to see this if you treat $(x^3 y^2)^2$ as $(x^3 y^2) \times (x^3 y^2)$ where you can add the indices.

11 (a)	$-2, -1, 1$	2
(b)		

x	-2	-1	0	1	2
y	8	2	0	2	8

1

2

Answers to Unit 2

Question	Answer	Mark
	$x = 1.52$	1
(c)	$-2.25, -0.55, 0.80$	3

Examiner's tip You will lose marks for solutions that are wrong or omitted. It will be difficult to read the result in part (b) to the accuracy shown here. The correct readings from *your* graph will be given the marks.

---

12 (a)	Tangent drawn at $t = 4$	1
	$42 \div 8 = 5.25$	1
	Units m/s^2	1

Examiner's tip Try to draw the tangent so that it touches at time $t = 4$. Take the measurements to calculate the gradient as large as the diagram will allow.

(b)	Attempt at area under curve up to 10 seconds	1
	$\frac{1}{2}(0 + 55) + 12 + 23 + 31 + 37 + 42 + 46 + 50 + 52 + 54$	
	(trapezium rule using 10 strips)	2
	$= 374.5$ or 370 m	1

Examiner's tip You could also have obtained this answer by using 5 strips or by counting squares.

13	$\frac{1}{2} \times 5 \times 0.95 + \frac{1}{2} \times 5 \times (0.95 + 0.9) + \frac{1}{2} \times 5 \times (0.9 + 0.55)$	
	$+ \frac{1}{2} \times 5 \times (0.55 + 0.2) + \frac{1}{2} \times 5 \times 0.2$	
	or $5 \times (0.95 + 0.9 + 0.55 + 0.2)$	2
	$= 13$ m^2	1

Examiner's tip This trapezium method gives an underestimate, as the shape is largely convex. The triangles/trapezia leave out some area on most strips. Accuracy would be improved with more (narrower) strips. Alternatively, you could count squares. Care would be needed in deciding on the size of the square and what it represented. For example, if you chose squares measuring 2 mm by 2 mm, the total would be about 550. Each square represents 0.025 m^2, giving 13.75 m^2.

Answers to Unit 2

Question	Answer	Mark

14 (a)

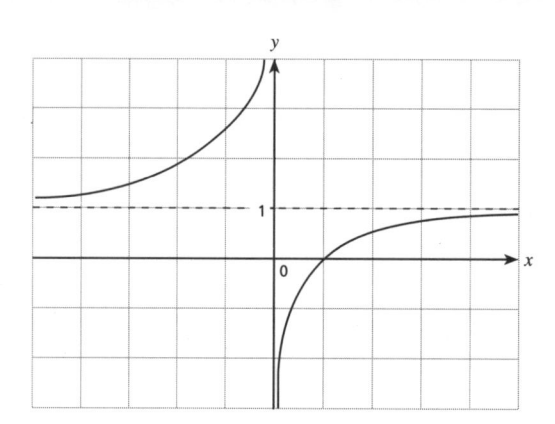

[Graph showing curve with horizontal asymptote y = 1 and vertical asymptote at y-axis]

2

(b)

[Graph showing curve with horizontal asymptote y = 1 and vertical asymptote at $x = -\frac{1}{2}$]

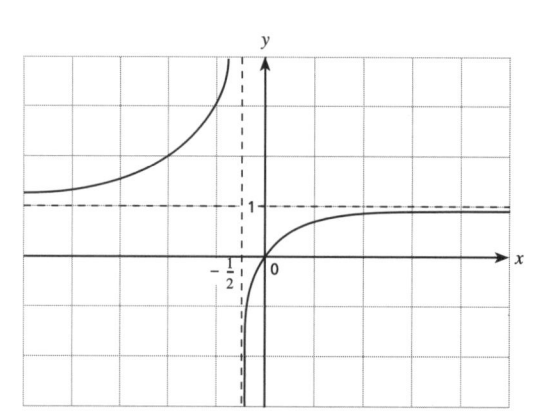

2

> **Examiner's tip** Sketching graphs of related functions requires you to think of the effect of replacing x by $x - 1$ or $2x$. In the first case, it is a translation 1 to the right and in the second a squash (stretch) factor $\frac{1}{2}$ in the x direction. Check the result matches the function, for example
> $f(2x) = \dfrac{2x}{2x+1}$ cannot be evaluated when $2x + 1 = 0$, that is when $x = -\dfrac{1}{2}$.

15

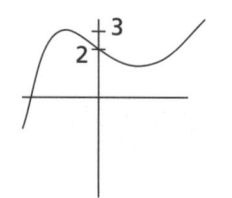

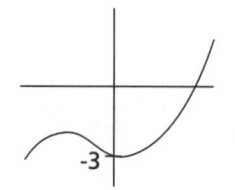

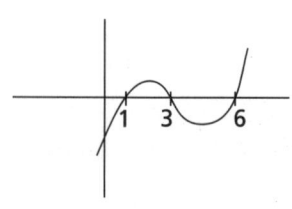

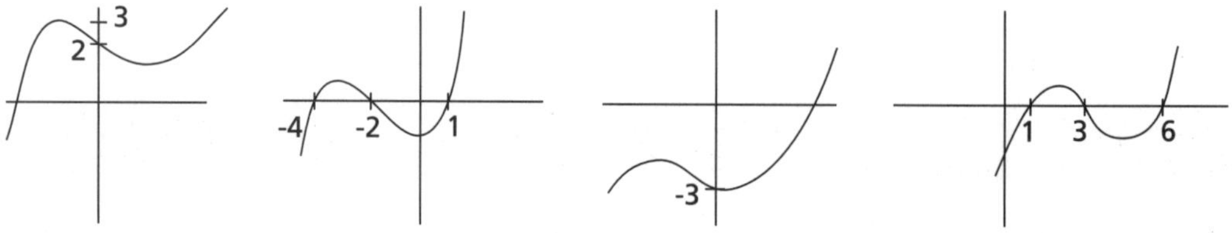

[Four sketch graphs: first with points at 2, 3; second with points at -4, -2, 1; third with point at -3; fourth with points at 1, 3, 6]

4
(one mark each)

> **Examiner's tip** Make sure you label any points on the axes of the sketches to show how the position has changed.

Answers to Unit 3

Question	Answer	Mark
16 (a)	−1.53, −0.36, 1.90	2
(b)	Line $y = 1 - x$ drawn.	1
	−1, −0.62, 1.62	2

Examiner's tip With care you can be accurate with the second decimal place. Although this question should be answered using graphical methods, it is possible to check your answer to part (b) using algebra. The graph shows that $x = {-1}$ is a solution, so $x^3 - 2x - 1$ can be written $(x + 1)(x^2...)$. By inspection, the quadratic factor is $x^2 - x - 1$ and solving the equation $x^2 - x - 1 = 0$ gives $x = 1.618...$, or -0.618. Don't spend time doing this in an examination – it earns no mark!

Question	Answer	Mark
17 (a)(i)	$\dfrac{x+2-x}{x(x+2)} = \dfrac{2}{15}$	1
	$\dfrac{2}{x(x+2)} = \dfrac{2}{15}$	1
	$x(x+2) = 15$	1
	$(x^2 + 2x - 15 = 0)$	
(ii)	$(x+5)(x-3) = 0$	1
	$x = 3$ or -5	1
(b)(i)	$\dfrac{x+1-x}{x(x+1)} = \dfrac{1}{x(x+1)}$	1+1
(ii)	$x(x+1) = 72$ $x = 8$	1

Examiner's tip As part (a)(i) starts with an equation, you could multiply both sides by $15x(x+2)$, giving $15(x+2-x) = 2x(x+2)$ as the first step. This does not work in part (b) (i), which is not an equation, and the $x(x+1)$ remains in the denominator.

3 SHAPE AND SPACE

Question	Answer	Mark
1	Scale factor for large ball from small ball = 3	
	Volume scale factor = 3^3	1
	27 small balls	1

Examiner's tip You can do this by working out the volumes using $\dfrac{4}{3}\pi r^3$ but this is unnecessary. It may help to think of how many 1 cm cubes will fit into a 3 cm cube:

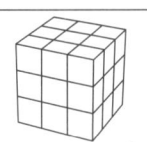

Answers to Unit 3

Question	Answer	Mark
2 (a)	$\dfrac{36}{30} = \dfrac{36-h}{10}$	1
	$12 = 36 - h \quad h = 24$	1+1
(b)	Slant height of complete cone $= \sqrt{36^2 + 15^2}$	1
	$= 39$	1
	Slant height of small cone $= \dfrac{1}{3} \times 39 = 13$	1
	Surface area of complete cone $= \pi \times 15 \times 39$	1
	Surface area of small cone $= \pi \times 5 \times 13$	1
	Surface area of shade $= 585\pi - 65\pi = 520\pi = 1634\,\text{cm}^2$	1
	(or 1630 cm² correct to 3 significant figures)	

Examiner's tip The first part is done using the ratios of corresponding sides in the similar triangles VDB and VCA. You need the formula for the curved surface area of a cone for the second part, $\pi r l$, where l is the slant height of the cone and r is the radius of the base.

3 (a)	$135 \times \dfrac{110}{90}$	1
	$= 165$	1
(b)	Area scale factor $=$ (linear scale factor)^2	1
	$\text{Cost} = 7 \times \left(\dfrac{110}{90}\right)^2$	1
	$= 10.456...$	1

Examiner's tip The answer to part (b) could be 10p or 11p, depending on economics! You must make sure you use the area scale factor. It was made clear in the question by stating that the price was proportional to the area.

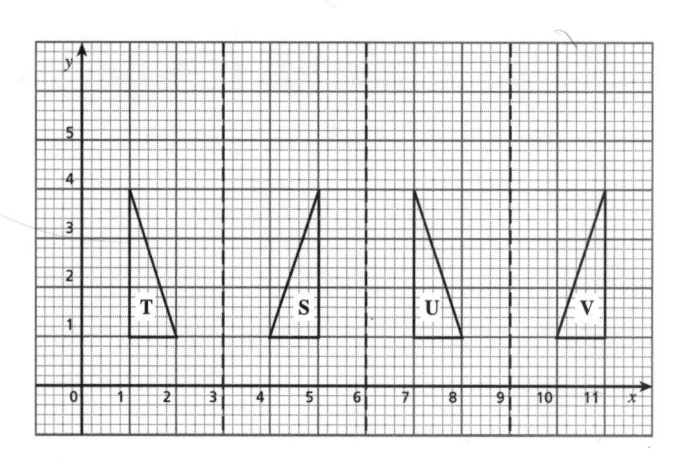

4 (a)		1

Answers to Unit 3

Question		Answer	Mark
(b)		Reflection in $x = 6$	1+1
(c)	(i)	Translation $\begin{pmatrix} 3n \\ 0 \end{pmatrix}$	1+1
	(ii)	Reflection in $x = \frac{3}{2}(n+1)$	1+1

Examiner's tip You should not need to draw any more triangles as the pattern can be extended from the four shown. For full marks you need to give all the details for each transformation.

---

5 (a)

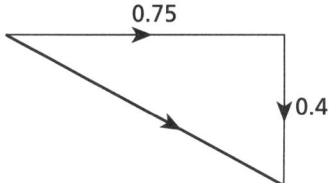

			Mark
	(i)	$\sqrt{0.75^2 + 0.4^2}$	1
		$= 0.85$ m/s	1
	(ii)	$\arctan \frac{0.4}{0.75}$	1
		$= 28.1°$	1
(b)	(i)	$\frac{15}{0.75} \times 0.4$	1
		$= 8$ m	1
	(ii)	$\frac{15}{0.75}$	1
		$= 20$ s	1

Examiner's tip The question allows accurate drawing in part (a) but the calculations are simple (and quicker!). Part (b)(i) can be found using 15 tan (answer to (a)(ii)) – it is the same calculation (although if you use the rounded answer it will not give exactly 8). The principle to be clear about is that each velocity in the vector triangle is applied to the *same time*.

6	(a)	$CD = 4$	1
		$? = 4 \tan 73°$	2
		$= 13.08$	1
	(b)	$? = \sqrt{13^2 - 4^2}$	2
		$= 12.37$	1
	(c)	Cosine rule: $130^2 = 169^2 + 169^2 - 2 \times 169 \times 169 \cos x$	2
		$x = 45.239...$	2
		$? = 169 \sin x$	1
		$= 120$	1

Answers to Unit 3

Question	Answer	Mark

Examiner's tip In parts (a) and (b), the symmetry of the isosceles triangles must be used to find the side of the right-angled triangle. Part (c) is not a symmetrical situation although you could use symmetry to start to solve the problem:

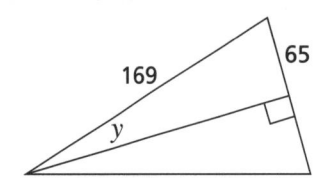

$y = \arcsin(65/169) = 22.619...$
$x = 2y = 45.239...$

7	(a)	1 to 50	1
	(b)	2.0	1
	(c)	$2.5^2 + 2^2$	1
		$= 10.25$	1
		$\sqrt{10.25} = 3.20...$ The pole is too long	1
	(d)	Width of shed $= 1.75$ m	
		Two longer positions:	

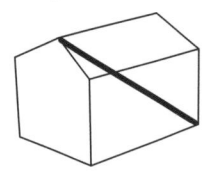

$\sqrt{2^2 + 2.5^2 + 0.875^2}$ 2

$= 3.3189...$ 1

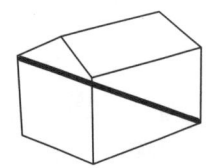

Height at side $= 1.5$ m

$\sqrt{1.5^2 + 1.75^2 + 2.5^2} = 3.400...$ 1

This is the longest.   1

Examiner's tip These solutions use the three-dimensional form of Pythagoras. You may prefer to build this up using the length of the diagonal of the base, or half the base of the shed. Which position gives the longest will depend on the relative dimensions of the shed.

8		Square joining centres has side 2 cm	1
		Diagonal of square $= \sqrt{2^2 + 2^2}$	1
		$= 2.828...$	1

Answers to Unit 3

Question	Answer	Mark
	Radius of container = small radius + half diagonal of square	1
	= 2.414 = 2.41	1

Examiner's tip You may find it helpful to draw your own diagram.

9 (a)	First high tide when $\sin(29.2t)° = 1$, i.e. when $29.2t = 90$	1
	$t = 3.082...$ hours: Time is 3.05 am (to nearest minute)	1

Examiner's tip Don't forget that there are 60 minutes in an hour, not 100!

(b)	First low tide when $\sin(29.2t)° = -1$, i.e. when $29.2t = 270$	1
	$t = 9.246...$ hours: Time is 9.15 am (to nearest minute)	1
(c)	$t = 24$, depth $= L + K\sin(700.8)° = L + (-0.3288...)K$	1
	The water level is lower on 2 July.	1

Examiner's tip Most calculators will find the sine automatically.

(d)	$t = 96$, depth $= L + K\sin(2803.2)° = L + (-0.9735...)K$	1
	$t = 96.1$, depth $= L + K\sin(2806.12)° = L + (-0.9606...)K$	1
	This is higher so the tide is rising.	1

Examiner's tip Care is needed with the last part since it is not far from low tide. A small difference in time, before or after, is required.

10	$AC^2 = 170^2 - 142^2$	1
	$= 8736$	1
	$AC = 93.46...$	1
	$AB = 2 \times AC = 186.9$ m	1

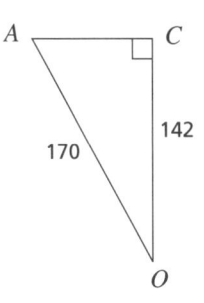

Alternative method:

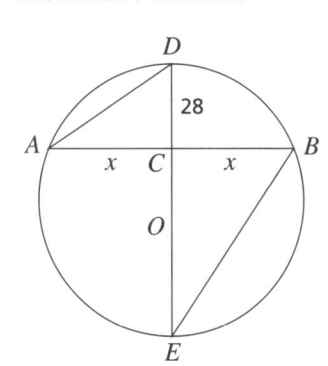

Using complete circle and diameter DE,
triangles ADC and EBC are similar — 1

$CE = 2 \times 170 - 28 = 312$ — 1

$AC = CB = x$

$\dfrac{x}{28} = \dfrac{312}{x}$ — 1

$2x = 2 \times \sqrt{8736} = 186.9$ m — 1

Answers to Unit 3

Question	Answer	Mark

Examiner's tip This shows two ways of tackling this problem. The first (and simplest on this occasion) uses Pythagoras and the other depends on similar triangles. The triangles are similar since angle DAB = angle DEB, subtending the same arc DB. Similarly angle ADE = angle ABE.

11 (a)

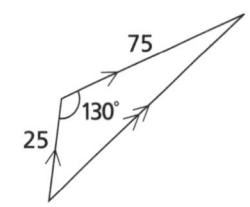

[Diagram: triangle with sides 25 and 75, included angle 130°]

Mark: 2

Examiner's tip It is worth marking the lengths and the angle since you will need them in the next part.

(b) Using cosine rule: (resultant)$^2 = 25^2 + 75^2 - 2 \times 25 \times 75 \times \cos 130°$ — 2

resultant = 93.1 — 2

Using sine rule: $\dfrac{93.06...}{\sin 130°} = \dfrac{75}{\sin x}$ — 2

$x = 38.1°$ — 2

Examiner's tip Write down the expressions you are going to evaluate in case you make an error.

12 (a) (i) $BQ = \sqrt{1.05^2 + 2.33^2}$ — 1

$= 2.56$ — 1

(ii) Angle $BQP = \arctan \dfrac{1.05}{2.33}$ — 2

$= 24.26°$ — 1

(iii) Arc $QS = \dfrac{2 \times 24.26...}{360}$ of full circle radius 2.56 m — 1

$= \dfrac{2 \times 24.26...}{360} \times 2 \times \pi \times 2.56...$ — 1

$= 2.16$ m — 1

(b) Area of end is sector SBQ + triangle SRB + triangle QBP — 1

$= \dfrac{2 \times 24.26...}{360} \times \pi \times 2.56...^2 + 1.05 \times 2.33$ — 2

$= 5.21$ — 1

Answers to Unit 3

Question	Answer	Mark

Examiner's tip The multiplier for the sector as a fraction of the whole circle is the same for area as arc length. The two triangles in part (b) are the same size and together make a rectangle. Answers may differ from these if you use earlier rounded answers.

(c) (i) $2.1 \times \dfrac{1}{19} = 0.1105$ m or 11.05 cm — 1

(ii) $5.21 \times \left(\dfrac{1}{19}\right)^2$ — 1

$= 0.0144$ m^2 or 144 cm^2 — 1

Examiner's tip Remember the area scale factor is squared and there are 10 000 cm^2 in 1 m^2.

---

13 (a) (i) $\mathbf{q} - \mathbf{p}$ (ii) $\begin{pmatrix} -1 \\ 2 \end{pmatrix}$ (iii) $\overrightarrow{SR}$ — 1+1+1

(b) (i) $\overrightarrow{RQ} = \overrightarrow{RO} + \overrightarrow{OQ}$ — 1

(ii) $\overrightarrow{SP} = \overrightarrow{RQ} = -\mathbf{r} + \mathbf{q}$ or $\mathbf{q} - \mathbf{r}$ — 1

Examiner's tip PQRS is a parallelogram so vectors along opposite sides are equal. This is used in parts (a)(iii) and (b)(ii).

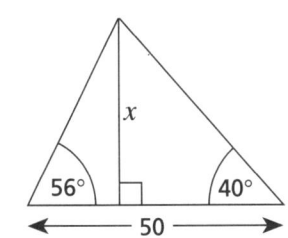

14

$\dfrac{x}{\tan 56°} + \dfrac{x}{\tan 40°} = 50$ — 3

$x(0.674... + 1.191...) = 50$ — 1

$x = 26.79$ m — 1

Examiner's tip The first three marks will be subdivided to give credit for the stages in obtaining the equation. Another method is to use the sine rule on the whole triangle.

---

15 (a) $AC^2 = 8^2 + 6^2$ — 1

$AC = \sqrt{100} = 10$ — 1

(b) $AC^2 = AV^2 + VC^2 - 2\,AV \times VC \times \cos AVC$ — 1

$\cos AVC = \dfrac{8^2 + 5^2 - 100}{2 \times 5 \times 8} = -0.1375$ — 1

Angle $AVC = 97.9°$ — 1

Answers to Unit 4

Question	Answer	Mark
(c)	Using the sine rule, $\sin VAC = \dfrac{5}{10}\sin AVC$ $(=0.4952\ldots)$	1
	$VN = 8\sin VAC = 3.96$	1+1

Examiner's tip Most calculators will give the obtuse angle for the negative cosine in part (b). The height in part (c) could have been found using the area of triangle AVC instead of the sine rule:
$\dfrac{1}{2} \times 8 \times 5 \times \sin AVC = \dfrac{1}{2} \times VN \times 10$

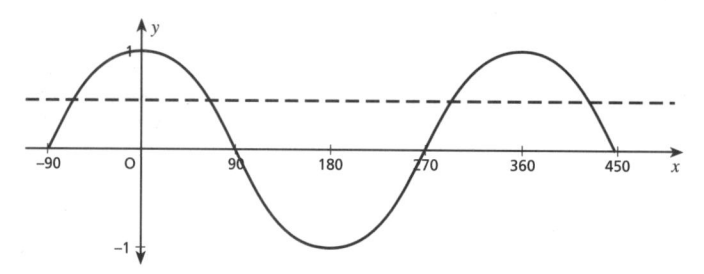

Question	Answer	Mark
16 (a)	[graph of sine curve from -90 to 450]	2
(b)	60	1
(c)	$-60, 300, 420$ (any two)	2

Examiner's tip Draw a line on your sketch to show where to find the other solutions and remember the symmetry of the graph.

4 HANDLING DATA

Question	Answer	Mark
1 (a)	(2), 5, 10, 15, 10, 8	1
(b)(i)	Many people will not shop in the morning or on Thursday.	1
(ii)	Ask people over several days at differing times.	1

Examiner's tip An area of 2 square centimetres on the histogram represents a frequency of 5 people.

Answers to Unit 4

Question	Answer	Mark

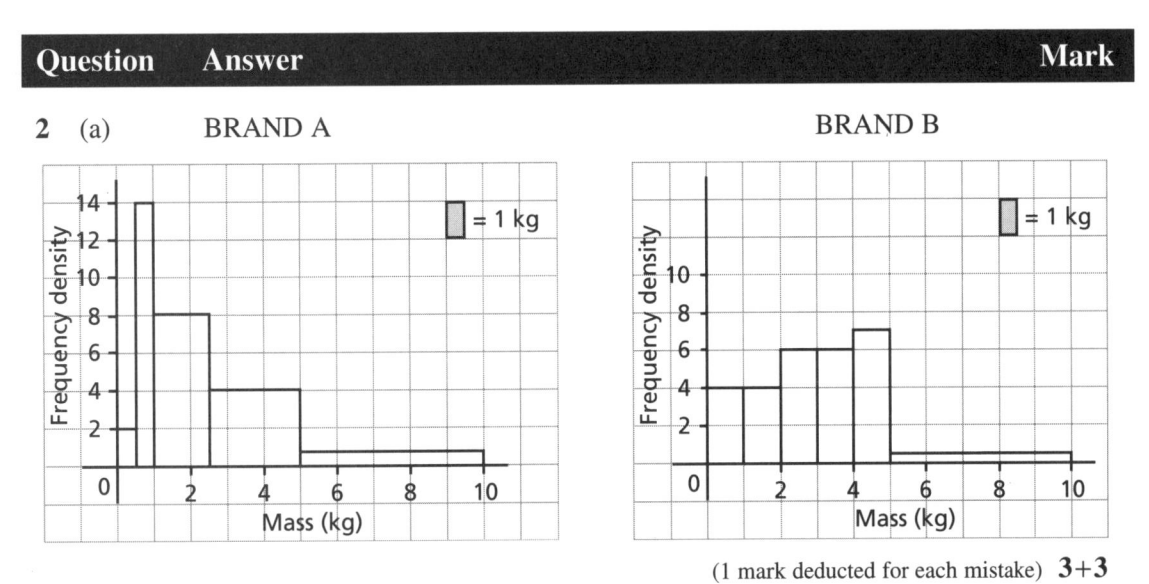

2 (a)   BRAND A   BRAND B

(1 mark deducted for each mistake) **3+3**

Examiner's tip The sizes of the classes vary in these distributions so the heights of the columns must be adjusted to make the area of the columns equal the frequency in each class. The axis up the page is Frequency density. You must decide on a unit area.

(b) Brand A mid-points: 0.25, 0.75, 1.75, 3.75, 7.5
Brand B mid-points: 0.5, 1.5, 2.5, 3.5, 4.5, 7.5   **1**

A	Mean: 2.62	SD: 1.93
B	Mean: 3.27	SD: 1.93

1+1

1+1

(c) Higher mean (better yield on average) from Brand B   **1**
Same spread (same degree of variation from the mean)   **1**

Examiner's tip A calculator with statistics makes these calculations much simpler and you would probably only have to do one in an examination.

Answers to Unit 4

Question	Answer	Mark

3

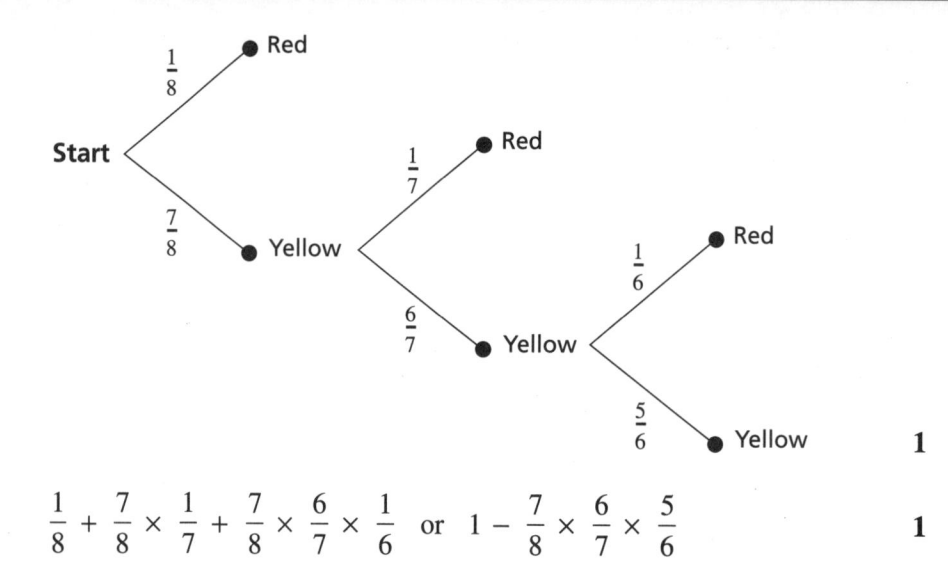

Tree diagram:
- Start → Red (prob $\frac{1}{8}$)
- Start → Yellow (prob $\frac{7}{8}$) → Red (prob $\frac{1}{7}$)
- Yellow → Yellow (prob $\frac{6}{7}$) → Red (prob $\frac{1}{6}$)
- Yellow → Yellow → Yellow (prob $\frac{5}{6}$)

Mark: 1

$$\frac{1}{8} + \frac{7}{8} \times \frac{1}{7} + \frac{7}{8} \times \frac{6}{7} \times \frac{1}{6} \quad \text{or} \quad 1 - \frac{7}{8} \times \frac{6}{7} \times \frac{5}{6}$$

Mark: 1

$$= \frac{3}{8}$$

Mark: 1

Examiner's tip Notice that there is no 'top' to the tree diagram as she stops as soon as she obtains a red. The alternative method is usually quicker. It is calculated as '1 − prob(no red)' and the outcome giving no red is when it is yellow every time.

4 (a) No – more boys than girls. — 1

(b) Sample 80 from 798 — 1

Approximately 1 in 10 — 1

Year 8: 15 pupils — 1

(or $80 \times \frac{150}{798} = 15$)

Examiner's tip This question is about choosing a stratified sample to represent the population for the survey. You were not asked for the number of boys and girls separately but 15 divided in the ratio 85:65 is 9:6 to the nearest whole number.

5 (a) Roast beef 0.6, fruit 0.2 — 1

(b) $0.6 \times 0.8 = 0.48$ — 1+1

Answers to Unit 4

Question	Answer	Mark
(c)	Probabilities right for main course	1
	sweet course	1+1

```
                       0.3  ── Fruit
         0.6   Roast beef ─<
                       0.7  ── Ice cream
        <
                       0.1  ── Fruit
         0.4   Vegetarian ─<
                       0.9  ── Ice cream
```

(d)	$0.6 \times 0.7 + 0.4 \times 0.9$	1+1
	$= 0.42 + 0.36 = 0.78$	1

Examiner's tip In part (c) there is one mark for each pair of probabilities right on the tree diagram.

---

6 Frequency Density scale should be marked 1 every 2 cm. — **1**

Column heights:
- 120 – 140   4 (given)
- 140 – 150   6
- 150 – 160   7
- 160 – 165   8
- 165 – 180   4

3

Examiner's tip The frequency density is measured in number of pupils per centimetre of height. You will lose 1 mark for each error.

			Mark
7 (a)	Probability (Double Fault)	$= 0.4 \times 0.05$	1+1
		$= 0.02$	1
(b)	Probability (Win)	$= 0.6 \times 0.75$	1
		$+ 0.4 \times 0.95 \times 0.5$	1+1
		$= 0.64$	1

Examiner's tip In part (b) Gabriella can win either with the first serve (0.6×0.75) or with the second serve if the first is not successful (0.4×0.95×0.5), the use of 0.4 earning the first mark.

Answers to Unit 4

Question	Answer	Mark

8 (a) (i) [Tree diagram: first branch $\frac{1}{6}$ Six, $\frac{5}{6}$ Not a six; second branch from Not a six: $\frac{1}{6}$ Six, $\frac{5}{6}$ Not a six; third branch from Not a six: $\frac{1}{6}$ Six, $\frac{5}{6}$ Not a six]   **2**

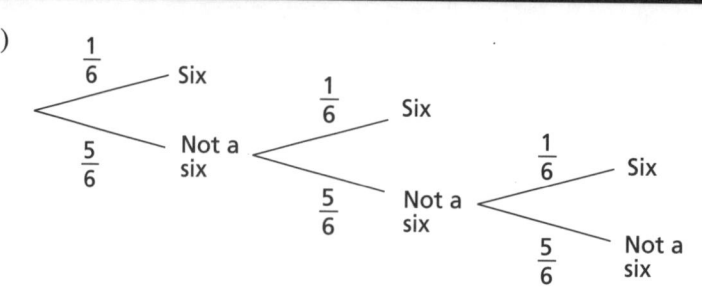

(ii) $\frac{5}{6} \times \frac{1}{6} = \frac{5}{36}$ **1+1**

(iii) Probability he wins = 1 − (probability he does not win)   **1**

$$= 1 - \left(\frac{5}{6}\right)^3 = \frac{91}{216} \text{ or } 0.421$$ **1+1**

> **Examiner's tip** Notice that the last part can be calculated from the probability he wins first throw, or the probability he wins second throw, or the probability he wins third throw, i.e.,
> $$\frac{1}{6} + \frac{5}{6} \times \frac{1}{6} + \frac{5}{6} \times \frac{5}{6} \times \frac{1}{6}$$

(b) (i) [Tree diagram: first branch $\frac{1}{6}$ Six, $\frac{5}{6}$ Not a six; second branch from Not a six: $\frac{1}{5}$ Six, $\frac{4}{5}$ Not a six; third branch from Not a six: $\frac{1}{4}$ Six, $\frac{3}{4}$ Not a six]   **2**

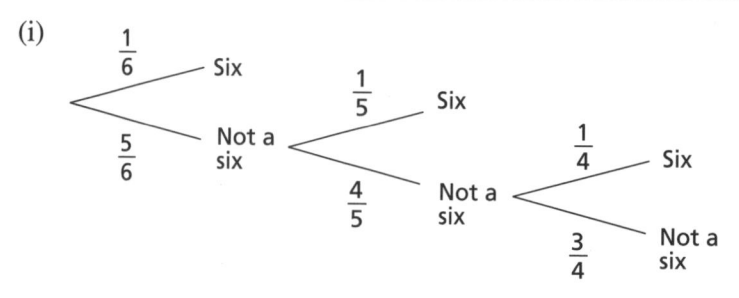

(ii) $\frac{5}{6} \times \frac{1}{5} = \frac{1}{6}$ **1+1**

(iii) $1 - \frac{5}{6} \times \frac{4}{5} \times \frac{3}{4}$ **1**

$= 1 - \frac{3}{6} = \frac{1}{2}$ **1+1**

> **Examiner's tip** The argument is the same as in part (a) except that conditional probabilities are used because the cards are not replaced. Note that you may have answered parts (iii) and (iv) the other way round.

(iv) As 3 cards are drawn, the probability that they contain the six is $\frac{3}{6} = \frac{1}{2}$.   **1**

9 (a) (i) $(28 + \ldots + 27) \div 10$ **1**

= 32 marks   **1**

Answers to Unit 4

Question	Answer	Mark
(ii)	$\sqrt{\frac{1}{10}(28^2+\ldots+27^2)-32^2}$	1
	= 11.9 marks	1
(b)	Boys' mean higher.	1
	Boys' scores more variable.	1

Examiner's tip The formula used here for the standard deviation is

$\sqrt{\dfrac{\sum x^2}{n}-\bar{x}^2}$ as it is not a frequency distribution.

Suitable formulae will be found at the front of the question paper. You may also use the statistics functions on your calculator.

---

10 Frequency Density scale marked or unit of area shown — 1

Column heights (see below) — 3

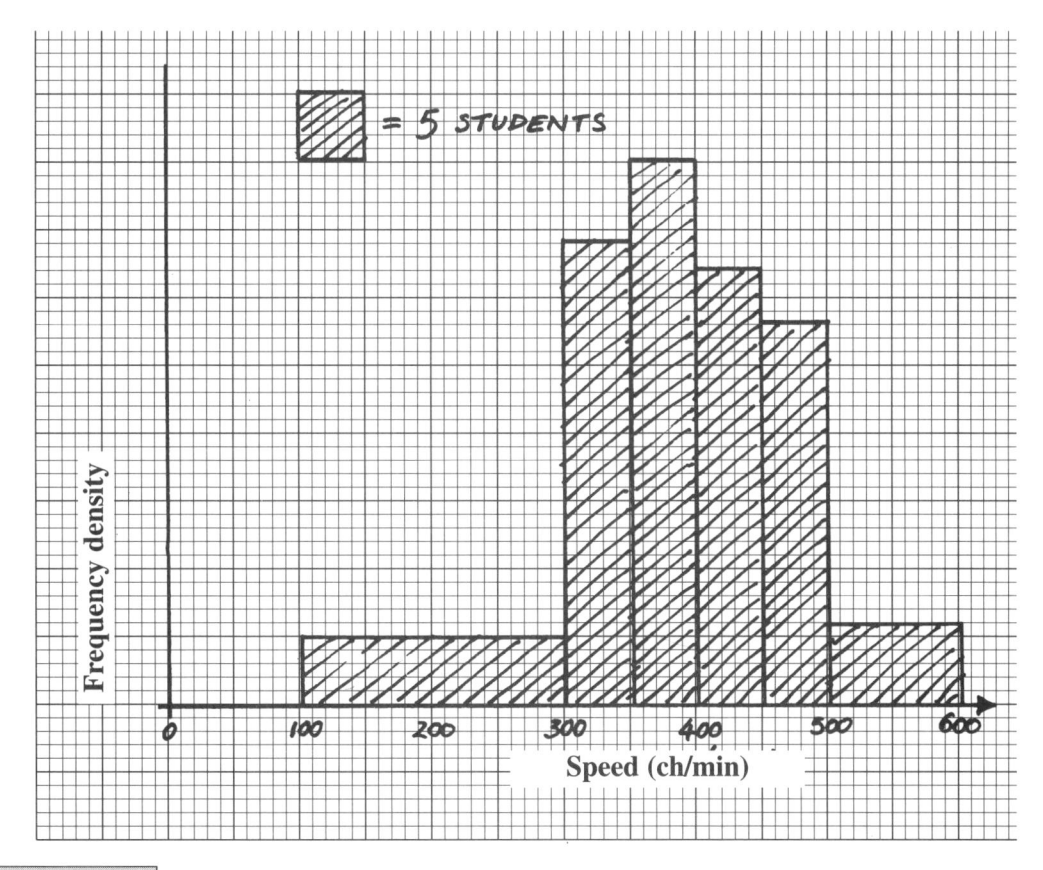

Examiner's tip If you choose a frequency density of one student per 5 characters/minute, the scale should be marked 1 for every 2 cm. In this case it is easier to use the alternative definition, choosing an area of 1 cm² to represent 5 students.

Answers to Unit 4

Question	Answer	Mark
11	Probability of at least one head = 1 − (probability of no head)	1
	Probability of no head in n tosses = $(0.5)^n$	1
	$1 − (0.5)^n > 0.95$	1
	$(0.5)^n < 0.05$	1
	$(0.5)^4 < 0.0625$, $(0.5)^5 < 0.03125$, so $n = 5$	1
12 (a)	Frequencies: 7, 6, 9, (16), (19), 36, (27).	4
(b)	Column width = 6 cm, column height 7.2 cm	2

Examiner's tip The easiest way to answer this question is to measure an area for which you know the frequency and work out the others by proportion.

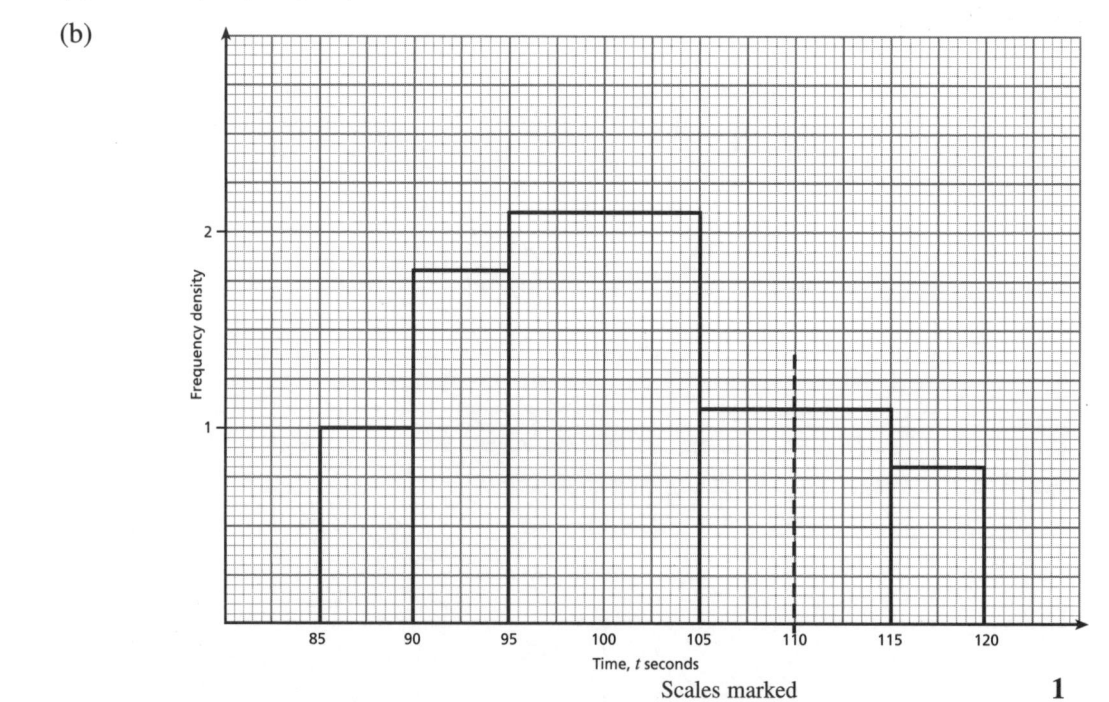

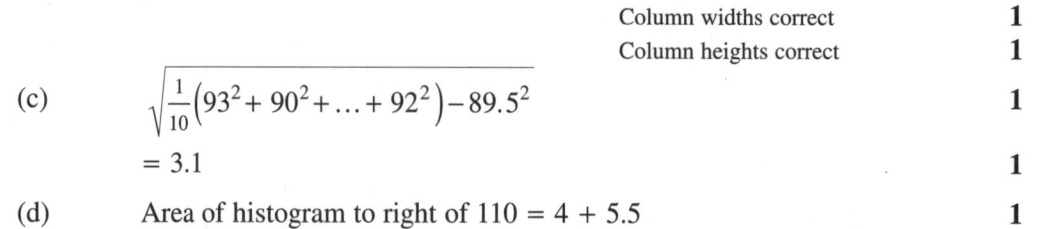

13 (a)	1, 1.8, 2.1, 1.1, 0.8	1
(b)	[Histogram with frequency density on y-axis and Time, t seconds on x-axis from 85 to 120]	
	Scales marked	1
	Column widths correct	1
	Column heights correct	1
(c)	$\sqrt{\frac{1}{10}(93^2 + 90^2 + \ldots + 92^2) - 89.5^2}$	1
	= 3.1	1
(d)	Area of histogram to right of 110 = 4 + 5.5	1
	Proportion = $\frac{9.5}{50}$ = 0.19	1

Answers to Unit 4

Question	Answer	Mark

Examiner's tip The frequency density has been found by dividing the frequency by the width of the class in each case. The result in part (d) is an estimate because we do not know how the times were distributed in the interval – they could all have been 105 seconds!

---

14 (a) $\dfrac{1}{8}$ **1**

   (b) $\dfrac{3}{8} \times \dfrac{1}{5} = \dfrac{3}{40}$ **1+1**

   (c)(i) $\dfrac{1}{8} \times \dfrac{1}{5} = \dfrac{1}{40}$ **1**

     (ii)   Probability (G secretary, B treasurer) $= \dfrac{1}{8} \times \dfrac{1}{3}$ **1**

          Probability (G and B) $= \dfrac{1}{8} \times \dfrac{1}{5} + \dfrac{1}{8} \times \dfrac{1}{3} = \dfrac{1}{15}$ **1+1**

Examiner's tip Make sure your fractions are right!.